FEBRUAR

TO ANGIE,

HAPPY BIRTHDAY & THANKS FOR
HELPING TO MAKE IT A FUN
WINTER!

NOW FOR SUMMER ...

LOVE FROM

Siân & Andy

THE SUMMER
SOLSTICE

THE SUMMER SOLSTICE

Celebrating the Journey of the Sun
from May Day to Harvest

JOHN MATTHEWS

Foreword by

CAITLÍN MATTHEWS

A GODSFIELD BOOK

First published in Great Britain in 2002
by Godsfield Press Ltd
Laurel House, Station Approach, Alresford
Hampshire SO24 9JH, U.K.

2 4 6 8 10 9 7 5 3 1

Designed for Godsfield Press by
The Bridgewater Book Company

Illustrations by *Sarah Young*
Picture Research by *Vanessa Fletcher*
Page make up *Sara Kidd* & *Barbara Theison*

Printed and bound in Hong Kong

ISBN 1-84181-134-3

The publishers wish to thank the following for the use of photographs:
AKG, London/Eric Lessing: pps.3, 39, 40, 41, 43TL, 97; **Carole Ballard:** pps.91, 94, 132; **The Bridgeman Art Library:** pps
26 Private Collection, 72 Birmingham Museum and Art Gallery, 108 British Museum, 111 William de Morgan/The de
Morgan Foundation,London, 131 Birmingham Museum and Art Gallery; **Cameron Collection:** pps.12, 47, 113;
Chris Castle: p.117; **Collections:** pps.14 Graham Burns, 74 Brian Shuel, 98 Brian Shuel, 99 Jarrold Publishing;
Corbis: pps.8/9 David Gallant, 11 Adam Woolfitt, 13T Gail Mooney, 15 Macduff Everton, 18L Vanni Archive, 18TR
Gianni Diagli Orti, 19 Michael S Yamashita, 21 Asian Art and Archaeology, 33 Bettman, 24 C and J Lenars, 27 Kea
Publishing Services, 36/37 Danny Lehman, 43TR + 44 + 45 Archivo Iconographico,SA, 48 Christine Osborne, 55
Mimmo Jodice, 64/65 Bettman, 67 Jim Richardson, 68 Araldo de Luca, 70 Niall Benvie, 73 Archivo Iconographico SA,
74 Robert Maas, 78 Richard Hamilton Smith, 84/85 Nathan Benn, 87 Ecoscene, 92, Robbie Jack , 94 Patrick Johns, 95B
Layne Kennedy, 112 Minnesota Historical Archives, 114 + 115 Hulton -Deutsch, 120 Michael Freeman, 121 Elizabeth
Whiting and Associates, 126/127 Philip Gould, 127 Patrick Ward, 135 David Muench, 136 Adam Woolfitt, 138 Red
Spiegel; **Corbis/Stockmarket:** pps 42, 77, 113R; **Paul Felix:** pps 79, 89; **Gettyimages:** pps 137 Image Bank, 141 Stone;
The Hutchison Library: pps 13B Andrey Zvoznikov, 88 Bernard Gerard, 118/119 John Hatt; **Glasgow Museums and Art
Gallery:** p.71 Sir Joseph Noel Paton:The Fairy Raid Carrying off a Changeling; **Madanajeet Singh/Sawai Man Singh
Museum, Jaipur:**p.20; **Hue Walker:** p116. Cover image courtesy of Corbis.

CONTENTS

Foreword

When we were children, the long summer days were full of endless outdoor games and playful celebrations of the natural world. There was time to lie in the long grasses and watch the beetle coachman wend his way between swaying flower stalks, or to lie on our backs on the warm earth listening to the far-above song of the invisible lark while we watched the great clouds galleoning across the blue sky. The sun shone down on us; each day showed us new connections between rock, tree, and creature, connections that insinuated themselves into our dreams and games.

Now that we are grown, the space for play and celebration has shrunk about our shoulders like a worn-out coat. Yes, we are bigger, but the playful space within us is radically diminished. Instead of being a daily re-creation, our recreation is often squeezed into the narrow space of an all-too-short week's holiday. We often forget that holiday means "holy day," a day set aside entirely for acknowledging the gods, a time that respects the creative cycles of work by making time to rest and enter more deeply into the sacred continuum of all that is. Without such meaningful remembrances, times when we celebrate the year's turning, we may also forget to exist in harmony with the living world and so fall out of tune with life itself.

Before religions were codified, before writing and civilization, our ancestors knew that survival meant acknowledging the elements of the natural world. The migrations of animals that supplied their needs, the growth of fruits and grains, the fluctuations of sea and river, were all dependent upon the season of the year.

Weather lore, seasonal signs, and the cycles of the heavens were way markers by which survival was ensured. Springtime was the season of mating; summer the season of growing; fall the busy season of harvest before the long season of winter, the time of rest and storytelling. Each of these seasons had its rhythms of welcoming preparation, ritual, or acknowledgment, and grateful offerings of thanks, that the eternal song of the year might never cease.

The two still points around which the year turns like a pair of interlaced spirals are the solstices—literally, "the sun's standstill"—when winter spills into summer, and summer into winter again. We rightly acknowledge these two pivotal stations of the year as momentous gathering times: in the heart of winter, we gather in the home as a family; in the heart of summer, we gather outside as a larger clan of related kindred. For researches into DNA and the human genome reveal that we are all related; the blood that flows in our veins has common ancestry.

Wherever our ancient ancestors made their homes, different forms of celebration and spirituality developed, yet the differences are not really so vast. The needs of the desert nomad, the mountain dweller, the folk of the seashore, and the keepers of the woodlands determine the way in which they see the sacred revealed: yet all live under one sun. The customs, dances, songs, and myths of both hemispheres reveal a fully developed understanding of the sun cycle, as well as an acknowledgment of the ritual obligation to give thanks for the light that warms and promotes growth in all life. Many of these customs are explored in this book.

Just as its twin volume, *The Winter Solstice*, tracked the descent of the sun from harvest to Midwinter and beyond into the light-bringing months of early spring, so this volume covers the sun's ascent from spring's manifestation to the glory that is Midsummer and on to the season of harvest. As before, meditations and celebratory opportunities are offered in these pages to encourage readers' personal rituals of sacred acknowledgment. This book invites readers to engage with the year, to be of it, rather than just reading about it, to reacquaint themselves with the cycles of the natural world as practitioners of life.

By exploring how we personally respond to the cycles and celebrations in the place we now live, we come authentically to a meeting with the guiding principles of life; we make our own contract, rather than living by guidelines defined by others. We begin to live in harmony with our own personal cycles of sowing and reaping, celebration and reflection. Whatever reconnects us to the sun circle and the singing, shining year also reconnects us to the joy, freedom, and playful spirit that we had as children and that we can enjoy once more as adults.

Caitlín Matthews
Autumn Equinox 2001

Chapter One

FIRES OF THE SUN

Sing, sing, sing for the morning,
Sing for the dawning of Midsummer's Day!

CAITLÍN MATTHEWS: MIDSUMMER SONG

Waiting for the Sun

It is June 22nd, Midsummer's Eve. In the great circle of Stonehenge, on Salisbury Plain, England, a group of white-robed Druids awaits the rising of the sun. It is intensely cold and light rain mists the circle of stones. The watchers huddle in blankets and thick coats. Despite the unseasonable weather, there is an air of expectation, of scarcely contained excitement. At last, around 4 A.M. faint gleams along the horizon herald the arrival of the sun. Then the first rays of light stream out across the landscape and strike the hele stone (from *helios*, the sun), a single slab set apart from the rest of the circle. One of the Druids comes forward, sets an ancient bronze horn called a dord to his lips, and blows a long mournful note. The other watchers join in with a hymn to the risen sun, which emerges slowly, staining the earth golden and warming the ancient stones.

To ensure the continuance of the seasonal round, ritual observances were devised.

This scene is happening today, but it could have taken place at almost any time over several millennia. All who are present are aware that others have stood where they now stand for Midsummers without number, quietly watching and waiting, as they have done, since the circle of stones was first erected around 2000 B.C.E.

The building of Stonehenge remains one of the great mysteries of human endeavor. It took many years and vast communal effort. Despite various theories put forward over the last decade, its purpose remains enigmatic. One fact, however, remains largely unchallenged. Stonehenge, like many other stone circles and standing stones throughout Europe, is aligned to catch the first rays of the Midsummer sun.

Stonehenge and other Midsummer monuments are part of a universal acknowledgment of the sun as a source of life, fertility, and good fortune. We may know a great deal more today about the physical nature of our native star, but our ancestors knew full well, as do we, that without its light and warmth, there would be no life.

For this reason, the sun has been worshiped as a god by peoples as far apart as Siberia and South Africa, North America and China. Midsummer ceremonies are enacted throughout the world, nearly all involving the lighting of fires to honor the sun's moment of greatest strength, and stories are told about the sun's importance in cultures as diverse as Mexico and India.

The celebrations of Midsummer are equal in every way to those that honor the Winter Solstice, the return of the Midwinter sun. These celebrations and stories, and the building of monuments like Stonehenge that honor the physical nature of the sun, remind us how important the sun was to our ancestors—not only at Midsummer but throughout the year—and how much of that early understanding has been passed on to us today.

A Heliocentric Universe

We have not always lived in a heliocentric universe. The Greek philosopher Aristarchus of Samos first proposed a sun-centered model of the universe around

200 B.C.E., but this concept was quickly dismissed by Aristotle. The idea languished until the sixteenth century, when the great astronomer Nicholas Copernicus (1473–1543) proposed that the planets revolved around the sun, rather than around the Earth as had previously been accepted. Despite support from such luminaries as Johannes Kepler (1571–1630) and Galileo Galilei (1564–1642), the theory of a heliocentric universe was considered implausible by the vast majority of Copernicus' contemporaries and by most astronomers and natural philosophers for another hundred years.

Disagreements between astronomers made no difference, however, to those for whom the sun was an object of veneration. Long before, when the world was still young, our ancestors watched the sky, looking for signs and asking questions about the nature of the sun's journey. Where did the sun go when it disappeared below the horizon? Would it return? Why did its light and heat strengthen and weaken over the course of the year? The importance of such questions was enormous in a world tied to a series of heavenly events and the effect they had upon the seasons, the times of rain and sun, planting and harvest.

Two dates in particular, the Summer and Winter Solstices, effectively divided the year into times of plenty and scarcity. To ensure the continuance of this seasonal round, ritual observances were devised, aimed at propitiating the elements, or the gods who stood behind them, and at protecting the harvest and livestock, and those who tended them, from bad luck and negative forces.

A circle of white-robed Druids awaits the rising of the Midsummer sun at Stonehenge in Wiltshire, U.K.

As Midwinter marked the death and rebirth of the new sun, Midsummer saw the rising of that sun to its zenith, followed by a gradual waning of its power as the year turned once again toward winter. The period between early May and the end of September was a festival of the sun in all its aspects, with rituals designed to encourage and draw upon its luminous

This diagram of the Copernican universe places the sun at the center—a theory that took another hundred years to become accepted.

power and to track its journey across the heavens. The first months of this period, between May Day and Midsummer, celebrated the sun and its plenty; while the days between Midsummer and harvest in late September focused on the sun as the source of life and the ripener of grain.

These ancient traditions continue to influence us today in ways of which we are scarcely aware. Even now, we find it more natural to walk *deasil* or "sunwise," following the path of the sun, rather than *widdershins* or "against the sun," which is widely believed to be unlucky. Despite fears about global warming and the widening hole in the ozone layer, despite health warnings about the dangers of unprotected exposure to the rays of the sun, in ways great and small, we still acknowledge the mystery of the Midsummer sun.

Calling Back the Sun

At Midwinter, fires were kindled to encourage the return of the sun. At Midsummer, similar fires celebrated the sun's attainment of its greatest strength. Lighting fires at these sacred times was a hugely significant act, because it was believed that even the tiny light of a human fire could help draw down the greater light of the sun. This link between human fires and the natural fires of the heavens helps explain the importance attached to the secret of fire among our ancestors and the power that was given to those who knew how to call forth flame.

Many myths, such as the story of the Greek hero Prometheus, hold that we had to steal fire from the gods themselves, so jealously were its secrets guarded.

Prometheus was the wisest of a race of ancient Titans, the gods before the gods in Classical Greece. The goddess Athena, at whose birth Prometheus assisted, taught him the secrets of architecture, navigation, astronomy, mathematics, and metallurgy, all of which he passed in time to humankind. But Prometheus' greatest gift was that of fire. It is said that he stole this fire from Mount Olympus by breaking off

right
Prometheus stole the fire of the sun for mankind. (The Rockefeller Center ice rink)

below right
A Russian shaman performs a dance to call the spirits.

a fragment of the fiery chariot of the sun and hiding it inside the hollow of a giant fennel stalk as he made good his escape. When Zeus learned of this act, the king of the gods punished Prometheus by chaining him to a pillar in the Caucasian Mountains where a vulture tore at his liver every day. But by then, humankind had received the gift of fire, and it could not be taken back.

From other tales, such as the Inuit story of Raven on pages 28–31, we hear of the need to win back the sun after it had been stolen away by those who coveted its strength. Many cultures also believed that it was necessary to propitiate the sun—to ensure its return by bribing it with gifts. Since without its light, death would soon follow, it was considered necessary to offer sacrifices—animal and even human—to bring about the restoration of the light.

Calling back the sun was one of the foremost tasks of the ancient wisdom keepers known as shamans. Like the Druids of Britain and Ireland, who served a similar function among the Celtic tribes, shaman-priests in cultures from Iceland to South America would climb to a high place and watch for the first show of light, greeting it with a call that announced to everyone that the sun had returned and the solstice could again be celebrated.

Festivals of Fire

Though the cultures that celebrated them were diverse, the ceremonies honoring the Summer Solstice had many common features. Most often these festivals centered on the lighting of fires, which served to purify the land and the people, to drive away negative forces, and to honor the sun.

Fire is a dramatic feature of the Beltaine celebrations at Calton Hill, Edinburgh, Scotland.

At the house where I was entertained, it was told me that we should see at midnight the most singular sight in Ireland, which was the lighting of Fires in honor of the Sun. Accordingly, exactly at midnight, the Fires began to appear: and taking the advantage of going up to the leads of the house, which had a widely extended view, I saw on a radius of thirty miles, all around, the Fires burning on every eminence which the country afforded. I had a further satisfaction in learning, from undoubted authority, that the people danced round the Fires, and at the close went through these Fires, and made their sons and daughters, together with their cattle, pass through the Fire; and the whole was conducted with religious solemnity.

Until comparatively recent times, huge, communal fires were still being lit in villages across Ireland. Local farmers considered it lucky if the smoke from these fires drifted across their land. Individuals also lit their own fires. Chains of these fires may still be seen in Ireland from May Eve to Midsummer Night. In Sweden a Midsummer Tree is set up and decorated for people to dance around, while in Norway, Germany, France, and Spain, Midsummer fires are still ignited with a sense of devotion that spans the ages.

Heavenly Cycles

The Celtic peoples of Northern Europe celebrated Midsummer by building great bonfires through which cattle were driven and over which couples jumped to ensure fertility in the coming year. A description dating from 1795 paints a vivid picture of these events. The writer, Reverend Donald McQueen, describes a visit to Ireland on Midsummer's Eve:

The word *solstice* comes from the Latin *solstitium*; literally, "sun stands still." The name recognizes that for approximately six days in June and again in December, the sun appears to rise and set at more or less the same point on the horizon, seemingly standing still in the sky for this period of time. This illusion is caused by the slight tilt in the Earth's axis in relation to the sun. A tilt toward the sun for the northern hemisphere brings summer; a tilt away, the chill of winter. The transition times between these orientations are the solstices. To our ancestors this alteration of the seasons was miraculous, a pattern that could cause disaster if it varied. Hence the sacred importance placed on the return of the sun each morning and seasonally each year.

More than any other heavenly body, the sun came to represent stability and cosmic order. The rhythm of its appearance every morning over the horizon, its traversal of the heavens, and its final disappearance over the edge of the world every night established a pattern that could be recognized wherever one was. Dawn and dusk were, as they are still, magical times—thresholds, gateways through which the sun passes again and again. The wonderful story overleaf dates from around 500 C.E. and comes from the Jewish Talmud; it illustrates the magic of these transition points perfectly.

In celebration of Midsummer Day, a cross-shaped pole stands on a farm at Skane, Sweden. (The festival celebrates the solstice and the birth of St. John the Baptist.)

One day, Rabba bar-Hana, a famous traveler of antiquity, was guided by an Arab to the edge of the world. At that place, which was really the horizon, everything seemed to come to an end, and the world fell away to nothingness. However, there was one window through which the movement of the planets could be observed. Arriving at the hour for evening prayer, Rabba placed his basket of food on the celestial window sill and prepared to pray. When his prayers were finished, he looked for the basket only to find it had gone.

"Who has stolen my food?" he demanded.

His guide replied, "While you prayed, the Wheel of the Heavens turned and the world moved on. Wait until tomorrow and it will return. Then you can eat."

What the sky plows under in the west will rise again in the east. Through the movement of the heavens, Rabba's dinner became his breakfast.

For our ancestors, the comings and goings of the sun were a constant reminder of the cyclicity of life itself. For us today, the cycles of the sun remind us that whatever is apparently lost can return to us, and that yesterday's experiences sow seeds that bear tomorrow's fruit.

Journeys of the Gods

Many of the myths and stories that attend the solstices tell of the journey of the sun across the heavens. From early times the two great dates of Midsummer and Midwinter were perceived as gateways for the soul on its journey into and out of life. This pattern was echoed by journeys undertaken by the gods, often on behalf of humankind.

In Egypt the sun god Ra passed through a heavenly portal, sailing his sun boat into the lower world at night, bringing light to imprisoned souls and battling against the monsters of the Underworld,

before returning, triumphant, with the dawn. The importance of the sun in Egyptian religious belief was immense. The story of Ra's epic journey and his triumphant return every morning were seen as metaphors for the journey of the human soul. As archeoastronomer E. C. Krupp memorably puts it:

We tell...sun stories about ourselves whenever we rechronicle the triumph of the light over dark. We see ourselves born; we watch ourselves grow; we witness our deaths; and we celebrate the new children who replace us...That's why the Egyptians put the sun story on the walls of a tomb. They and many other peoples have believed that we complete the cyclical tale and put it in motion again by dying and transcending death through resurrection, reincarnation or some other transformation...that carries us from the darkness into the light. (Beyond the Blue Horizon)

This same theme found expression in Northern Europe, where for the Norse people the sun emerged every day through Deling's Dore (Dawn's Door) after a struggle with the gods of night and the abyss. On the far-off Pacific coast of Canada, the Bella Cool Indians also speak of gates of dusk and dawn guarded by a giant warrior named the Bear of Heaven, who allows the sun to pass through, but no one else.

Elsewhere, in the myths of Mesopotamia, we hear of Shamash, the god of the sun, entering and exiting through gates guarded by monsters. Stepping through the Gate of the East onto the Mountain of Sunrise, he toils through the day until he reaches the Mountain of Sunset, from which he passes through the Western Gate of heaven. There he meets with his wife, sits down for a meal, and rests before beginning the cycle again the next day. The cycle of life reflects the daily life of humankind.

right
The Egyptians revered many gods who
represented the sun. This tomb painting depicts Ra,
with the falcon's head, and Aten, to the left.

below
When the Midsummer sun aligns with the Temple
of Amun at Karnak, Egypt, a beam of
light is channeled to the heart of the complex.

Temples of the Sun

Many ancient temples were designed to celebrate the moment when the sun first showed above the horizon on the longest day of the year and to recall the journey of the god. In Egypt temples dedicated to the falcon-headed sun god Amon-Re were designed to capture the sun's rays at the exact moment of the solstice. At the great temple at Karnak, a concentrated beam of light is channeled at Midsummer into the heart of the complex, enabling the priests to calculate the duration of the solar year to within a minute, a degree of accuracy we have only recently learned to match.

But surely the most astonishing and important sun temple is the vast complex of Ankor Wat in present-day Cambodia. Built somewhere between 1113 and 1150 C.E., this temple represents one of the largest and most complex astronomically based buildings in the world. Measuring almost a mile across in each direction, it was designed both as a tomb for its builder, King Suryavarman II, and as a celestial observatory. A group of astronomers who studied the site in 1976 declared that virtually every measurement within the complex has calendrical information encoded within it.

The sun was of immense importance to the builders of Ankor Wat, so much so that the bas-reliefs that decorate nearly every available surface are oriented toward the sun. The exact moment of the Midsummer sunrise can be observed from the western gate of the complex. The vast frieze depicting the birth and creation of the world receives the blessing of the sun's rays every day, signifying, it is believed, the relationship between the human world and the vastness of the universe.

The whole complex is, perhaps, the finest example of two themes that run through much of the symbolism of the solstices: that the world is controlled by cosmic forces, and that only by acknowledging and propitiating the figures who represent these forces can harmony be preserved. The honoring of the sun at its high point, it was believed, was essential to the continued health of the cosmos and to humankind's continued existence within the cycles of nature.

The impressive remains of Ankor Wat in Cambodia show literally hundreds of carvings oriented toward the sun.

Eastern Festivals of the Sun

As celestial temples such as Ankor Wat remind us, the religious cultures of the East also placed great emphasis on the solstices and other cosmic events.

This seventeenth-century piece of silk embroidery from Rajasthan, India, depicts the god Krishna surrounded by cows, which represent the sun's rays.

Early Hindu people had considerable astronomical knowledge, though Brahmin priests believed the Earth to be flat, with a sacred mountain rising from the center, around which the sun and the planets revolved. Nearly all of the major Hindu deities were associated with the sun, especially Vishnu, Varuna, and Surya. In the ancient Sanskrit text, the *Rig Veda*, cows are identified with the sun's rays and the solar deity Krishna is their divine protector.

Across much of the Indian continent elaborate festivals celebrated the passages of the solar year. These ceremonies, designed principally to identify the precise moments of solstices and equinoxes, included the lighting of fires and profound sacrificial events, aimed at a spiritual reenactment of the creation of the universe.

Sophisticated astronomers, the Chinese were making detailed maps of the heavens at least as early as 1500 B.C.E. For them the year was divided into quarters, bounded by the solstices and equinoxes. They calculated the dates of these events precisely by taking measurements from a gnomon or sun-stick, which cast its shadow across a marked circle according to the position and height of the sun. The solstices were marked by important festivals, during which the emperor led the people in prayers and offerings. The Winter Solstice celebrated the masculine, or yang, energies; while

Midsummer honored and encouraged the feminine, or yin, forces. The Midsummer festival was celebrated at the square-shaped Altar of the Earth, which lay a little way outside the northern walls of the Forbidden City. During the festival a sacrifice—at one time certainly human—was offered to the fire, the smoke rising toward the sky seen as a link between heaven and earth.

Japanese knowledge of the heavens drew on Chinese traditions. One of the most important Japanese deities is Amatarasu, the goddess of the sun. She is one of the primal gods from whom the emperors of Japan

The Japanese sun goddess Amatarasu hid herself in a cave from which she was lured forth by the dancing and singing of the other gods.

were believed to have descended. In the seventh century, a priest named Mim was sent to China to study astronomy. On his return he set up Japan's first observatory at Asuka, from which the first sighting of Halley's Comet was recorded some hundred years before the birth of Edmund Halley. All that remains today of the observatory are two great carved megaliths, one of which has a series of incised markings on its surface precisely oriented toward the solstice and equinox sunsets.

Now is the month of maying,
When merry lads are playing
Each with his bonny lass
Upon the greeny grass.
Fa la la!

The spring clad all in gladness
Doth laugh at winter's sadness,
And to the bagpipe's sound
The nymphs tread out their ground.
Fa la la!

Fie then, why sit we musing,
Youth's sweet delight refusing?
Say, dainty nymphs, and speak,
Shall we play barley-break.
Fa la la!

Thomas Morley

Rituals of the Sun

On the American continent as well, the power of the sun's journey and the importance of the solstice was acknowledged. At Chaco Canyon, New Mexico, a series of petroglyphs carved high on the rock face of Fajada Butte record the passage of the sun through the solstices and equinoxes. The mysterious Anasazi people of North America responsible for these carvings, whose culture flourished between 1300 and 400 B.C.E., possessed a highly developed knowledge of the solar calendar. They passed on at least some of this knowledge to their descendants, the Hopi and Zuni peoples, who still celebrate the turnings of the year with elaborate festivals.

Among the Zuni, the *Pekwin*, or "Sun Priest," conducted these events, which began with watching for the return of the sun from a small tower at the edge of the village. When the solstice was announced, complex ceremonies took place, in which masked Kachina priests enacted spirit dances, the steps of which had been handed down for generations. Among their cousins, the Hopi, whose agricultural as well as

The Mississippian chiefs bore the title "Great Sun" and were acknowledged as human brothers of the god.

ritual year was governed by the passage of the sun, it was said that at the time of the Summer Solstice, the spirit people represented by these dancers returned from the lower world, where it was still winter, passing through the Earth on a journey up into the mountains, where they would commune with the dead. Thus a form of balance was preserved, the light and dark periods of the year mirroring the passage of the Kachinas from the lower world to the upper. These spirit dances may still be observed today, though the native people are fiercely protective of their mysteries.

In the eastern half of North America, where the Mississippian culture flourished from approximately 750 to 1500 C.E., the journey of the sun was witnessed from the pyramidal mound known as the St. Louis Gateway Arch, or Monk's Mound, which rises from the fertile plain of the Mississippi Basin. At one time, the mound was adorned by a sun temple.

Archeological evidence tells us that the sun was supremely important to the Mississippians. Their chiefs bore the title "Great Sun" and were acknowledged as human brothers of the sun god. Thus the chieftains also acted as priests and perhaps lived in houses atop the mound, a symbol of their social and spiritual status. Archeologist Warren Wittry has discovered a number of post holes arranged in circles in a field near the mound. Dubbed the "American Woodhenge" or "Sun Circle," this site continues to be the subject of speculation. Many believe that the post alignment was a way of measuring the sun's path through the sky, with special attention to the solstices, as at Stonehenge.

At the moment of the Summer Solstice a beam of light enters the "Cave of Life" in Arizona's Petrified Forest.

Sacrifices to the Sun

In Central America, the Aztecs, Mayans, and Toltecs celebrated the importance of the Summer Solstice by building great temples aligned to the moment of the sun's rising. At what is perhaps the greatest surviving Mayan city, Chichén Itza, the Caracol or Spiral Tower has windows and doors oriented to the setting and rising sun at both solstices and equinoxes. Elsewhere, at Uaxactún, in the rainforest of Guatemala, a viewing platform on one the largest buildings enables a watcher to see the sun rise over a series of smaller pyramids built in exact alignment with the great solar event. Evidence collected from the descendants of the Mayans suggests that they had shaman-priests known as "daykeepers" and "sunkeepers" whose task it was to study the heavens and to measure and record the cycles of the sun.

The Toltecs, who overran much of the Mayan world around 900 C.E., adopted many of the conquered race's traditions regarding the significance of the sun and the stars. The Aztecs, who came later still and built upon the beliefs of both earlier peoples, came to interpret the life of the sun in a particularly violent way. To them the sun had to be propitiated to ensure that it returned from below the horizon. This propitiation was accomplished through the sacrifice of hundreds of people each day. The victims were made to ascend the steps of the pyramid at the great city of Tenochtitlán where their still-beating hearts were torn from their breasts and shown to the sun.

Farther south, the Inca people also built astonishing temples, many of them dedicated to the sun. At the Incan capital, Cuzco, the principal temple building was the Coricancha, or Temple of the Sun, oriented toward the Midwinter sunrise (see page 27). The temple site is

The seventh-century Temple of the Sun from the ancient Mayan city of Planque, Mexico.

probably related to an Inca creation myth that holds that the first children of the sun god were sent to Earth to find a place to set up the golden rod that their father had given them. This rod was almost certainly a kind of gnomon, or measuring stick. It may also have represented the rays of the sun at its zenith on Midsummer Day.

A description from around 1600 describes the ritual use of these gnomons. The columns were observed with great care and attention until, at midday, "the sun bathed all sides of the column and cast no shadows at all...Then [the people] decked the columns with all the flowers and aromatic herbs they could find and placed the throne of the sun [there]... saying that on that day the sun was seated on the column in all his full light."

Sun Dancing

Among the Native Americans of the North American Plains the sun was regarded as the greatest manifestation of the Great Spirit. A number of ceremonies grew out of this belief, the most famous of which was the Sun Dance at the time of the Summer Solstice. This ritual observance was designed to test the mettle of the young warriors who performed it and to bring them visions.

Preparations began with prayers for fair weather. These were followed by the ceremonial cutting and stripping of a huge tree by four impeccable youths and virgins. Prayers were led by the tribal shaman, the pole was painted, and the dancing ground prepared. When all was ready, the pole was raised, accompanied by tobacco offerings and a begging dance to request the favor of the Great Spirit.

The dance itself lasted between one and four days, during which time the participants abstained from food and drink. On the first morning, dancers took a sweat bath and painted their bodies in symbolic colors: red for sunset, blue for the sky, black for

the night. The dancers then donned deerskin aprons, rabbit-fur wristlets and anklets, and plaited feathers into their hair. In their mouths, they carried bone whistles decorated with porcupine quills and eagle down. The dancers circled in procession, stamping on the balls of their feet to the beat of a large drum, while special songs were chanted.

The primary object of the dance was personal dedication to the sun and the Great Spirit. Participants demonstrated these vows through endurance and pain. In some instances they lacerated their arms and thighs. Others suspended themselves from the pole by ropes attached to their flesh by bone pins skewered though gashes in their breasts or backs, so that only their toes touched the ground. The ceremony continued until the dancers fell unconscious or tore themselves loose. Many received a vision during the proceedings. After a prescribed duration, they were given food and water; then they smoked the sacred pipe and took a vapor bath.

above
This painting shows the Sun Dance ceremony of the Mandan people of North America.

right
Part of the circular wall that surrounds the Inca Sun Temple at Cuzco, Peru. (The Church of San Domingo, which now stands within the wall.)

The Theft of the Sun

Countless folk stories have come down to us that develop the mythology of the sun, especially as it relates to the needs of human beings. Many of these tell of the theft, or loss, of the sun and its recovery by various gods and heroes. A story from the Inuit people of northern North America tells us how a particularly cunning folk hero recovered the light from a greedy guardian.

Raven and the Theft of Light

*I*n the beginning everyone lived on this side of the sky. But one day the great magician Tupalik decided to find out what lay on the other side. So he cut a hole and climbed through. He so liked what he found there that he decided to build a house and take up residence.

But Tupalik's wife was not happy. She missed all her friends and felt lonely. So Tupalik decided to cheer her up by stealing the light. He climbed through the hole in the sky, seized the sun and moon, and thrust them into two bags. Then he returned home and hung the bags from the roof.

After that Tupalik let the light out only when he felt like it, and in the the rest of the world people began to grow thin and pale from lack of light. Eventually they went in search of Raven, who had helped before. "Raven, someone has stolen the moon and the sun. We are dying for lack of light! Please, can you try to get it back for us."

Raven agreed and then he thought hard. "I'm sure Tupalik has something to do with this," so he flew off across the world until he saw the hole in the sky and went through it. He found Tupalik dozing under the sun, which he happened to have let out that day.

"Hey, Tupalik," said Raven, "I want the sun and moon back."

But Tupalik shook his head. "I need them to cheer up my wife. Besides, I like them too much to let them go."

Raven flew off and thought of ways that he might steal back the sun and moon. He saw a beautiful maiden going to fetch water from the river. Raven knew she must be Tupalik's daughter. An idea came into his head. With a chuckle he flew down to the river's edge and turned himself into a feather floating on the water.

Tupalik's daughter filled her jug and didn't notice when the feather floated inside. She didn't notice the feather slipping down her throat later when she took a drink. But, a few months later, she gave birth to a baby boy.

Tupalik and his wife were delighted by their grandson, not knowing he was really Raven in disguise. They doted so much on the baby they gave him everything he asked for. And Raven made sure that he was always asking for something, yelling at the top of his lungs every day.

One day he started crying for the bags with the sun and moon in them. Tupalik was away hunting. At first his wife and daughter ignored the baby. But soon they got so sick of hearing him cry and scream that they gave him the bag with the moon in it to play with. When they weren't looking Raven unknotted the bag, and the moon flew out and vanished through the smokehole.

When Tupalik came home he was furious. But when he saw his grandson smiling and peaceful he eventually relented. "After all, I still have the sun," he said.

Soon the old wizard settled down to sleep, and at once Raven began to scream and cry for the bag containing the sun. Tupalik, weary and wanting sleep, told his wife to give the baby anything as long as it calmed him down.

So Tupalik's wife took down the bag and gave it to the baby. As soon as she was looking the other way, Raven ran outside and turned back into his own shape. The bag was tied too tight for him to open it, so Raven had to fly back through the hole in the sky carrying the bag in his talons.

The moon was back in the sky by this time, having floated out through the hole in the sky, and the people had begun to resume their lives somewhat, though they still missed the sun.

Soon Raven grew tired from carrying the heavy bag. He spied some fishermen below him.

"Please give me some fish," he cried. "I'll let the sun out if you do."

Now Raven had been gone so long that the people had forgotten that they had asked him to steal back the sun. The fishermen were reluctant to give him anything. Raven pecked angrily at the bag, and a few bright spots of light flew out and became the stars.

"Maybe he does have the sun," the fishermen said, and they gave Raven some food.

As soon as he was strong enough, Raven tore open the bag and out flew the sun. At first, everyone was blinded by the light, but after a while, they grew used to it and threw a huge party for Raven to thank him.

As for Tupalik and his family, some say that they moved back to this side of the sky. But others say they are still on the other side, and that every now and then Tupalik manages to steal back the sun for a while. But it always seems to get away.

This story of the trickster god Raven illustrates how the tremendous light and energy of the sun inspired the development of the human imagination. Inevitably, such primal forces acquired faces, personalities, stories. The Summer Solstice is a time for gods and spirits about whom many fascinating stories were told. The next chapter looks more closely at some of these.

Creating a Midsummer Shrine

Creating a shrine dedicated to the solstice can become a focal point for your personal celebration of Midsummer. What follows is a suggestion, based on a shrine in my own home.

❧ As a background for the shrine, create a banner representing the sun in its summer splendor. Alternately, find a painted image of a sunscape or an appealing piece of poster art. Other decorations might include a papier-maché sun, either handmade or purchased, candles, natural objects, plants, and flowers.

❧ A fireplace and its mantel is an ideal site for a solstice shrine. Since the weather is likely to be warm, instead of a fire, decorate the fireplace with leaves, flowers, and greenery. Then, either within the grate or in front of it, place a large glass bowl filled with water in which you arrange floating candles. Drape garlands of leaves and flowers along the mantelpiece, allowing them to trail down on either end.

❧ If you wish, place images or objects connected to the solstice around the fireplace. These may include representations of gods or goddesses associated with the solstice or the sun (see Further Reading for more information on books about deities) or natural objects, such as sunstones or crystals, the color of which suggests the warmth of the sun. Images that you make yourself can be even more meaningful than those you purchase. Honor your own sensibilities and taste in what you include.

❧ Once your shrine is complete, make it the focus of your spiritual practice in the days before and after the solstice. Do one of the meditations from this book, such as "Journey to the Sun," pages 60–62. Or contemplate the nature of the solstice, the beneficial energies and empowerment it brings to your life. You might even wish to offer a few words to the bounty of the sun, as our ancestors did. One such prayer might be:

I welcome the sun into my life
And give thanks for its daily bounty:
For its warmth to bless me,
For its strength to empower me,
For its light to illuminate my way.
I do this in the knowledge
That its light is also the light
Of wonder and holy wisdom,
Blessings I make welcome
In the pattern of my days.

❧ How long you choose to maintain your Midsummer shrine is up to you, of course. You might set it up a few days before the solstice, inaugurate it on the actual day, and then keep it active for a few more days. Be sure to keep the shrine fresh and clean, replacing old flowers or spent candles. Needless to say, always take care with lit candles, even in water, and never leave them burning when you are absent.

Knowing the Darkness, Knowing the Light

Use the night of the solstice to get to know the darkness so that you really appreciate the rising of the sun.

Turn out your lights. Unplug the TV, the computer, the electric clock. Unplug or switch off anything else you can. Light a candle inside. Then go outside and breathe in the night air. If it's raining, turn your face up to feel it. If you can, light a fire. Go for a walk in the night. Tell stories to friends, or read to yourself. Eat simple foods, or bake potatoes in the fire. Sit in silence for a time.

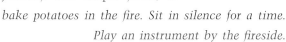

Play an instrument by the fireside. Sing a song and get others to join in. Doze by the fire in a blanket. Then, wake up before the first light and greet the sun as it climbs above the horizon. Feel the presence around you of all the people who have waited to greet the Midsummer sun through the ages. Be present to the moment and relish the sun's rising power. Sing a dawn song of honor and welcome, such as the Midsummer Song here:

Dark is the night, far is the dawning,
Sing for the shining of light on the way
Hearken, be ready, attend to our calling.
Sing all you guardians who wait at the door.

Chorus:
Sing, sing, sing for the dawning
Sing for the midnight, the noon, and the day!
Sing, sing, sing for the morning
Sing for the glory of Midsummer's Day!

Some say that wisdom is born of believing
Sing for the shining of light on the way.
Some say that wisdom is born of deceiving,
But wisdom shines bright in the dark or the day.

(Chorus)

Stones they were standing when starlight was breaking,
Sing for the shining of light on the way.
The seas and the rivers attend their own courses
When sunlight and moonlight upon them do play.

(Chorus)

The old times returning, the new times restoring,
Sing for the shining of light on the way.
From the beginning the Old Ones are singing
The song of the shaping that welcomes this day.

(Chorus)

CAITLÍN MATTHEWS

Chapter Two

GODS AND HEROES OF SUMMER

Sun shone from the south on the world's bare bones—
then was Earth o'er grown with herb of green
Sun, Moon's companion, out of the south…

THE ELDA EDDA

The Sun on the Stones

Everything about the sun encourages us to perceive it as godlike. From the beginning of recorded history, the sun has symbolized glory, power, brilliance, vitality, the animation of the soul. In Egyptian mythology, as in many creation stories, there was no life until light appeared, and since the sun was the source of light, it was also the source of life.

Before the written word, the earliest expressions of the idea of the sun's divinity are the carved petroglyphs found in many parts of the world. The earliest carvings date from the Stone Age, though the practice continued until the end of the Bronze Age and even into more recent historical time. Across much of Europe, especially in the area of present-day Scandinavia, thousands of such pictures have been discovered. Many focus on the worship of the sun, which is portrayed as a wheel or, as in ancient Egyptian myth, as a sun boat. Many carvings depict figures in attitudes of celebration and worship. A few hundred miles away, in Ireland, many rock carvings have been discovered in and around the

From the beginning of recorded history, the sun has symbolized glory, power, and brilliance.

These inscribed stones from Knockmany, Co. Tyrone, Ireland, display an ancient fascination with sun imagery.

This Bronze-Age artifact from Northern Europe depicts the chariot of the sun.

great Neolithic chambered tombs. Here, though there are no recognizable figures, the carvings clearly represent the sun in its various aspects from rising to setting and at different times of the year. These carvings underscore how important it was to early cultures to observe the sun, especially at the solstices, and suggest that the sun's significance was acknowledged both by worship and by precise astronomical observation.

Many Bronze-Age carvings show the sun disk being pulled along on a cart. Corresponding to these carvings, ritual objects, including bronze sun disks, have been discovered in Scandinavia and the Celtic countries. These suggest that people observed a ceremony in which carts carrying a sun disk were pulled along as a ritual enactment of the passage of the sun. Many of these disks are plain bronze on one side and gilded on the other, representing, perhaps, the sun's day side and night side. We might imagine that on ceremonial days, worshipers gathered at noon to observe a cart drawn past showing the sun's gilded side in imitation of the sun at its zenith. At sunset, the cart would pass again, showing the plain face of the sun disk. In later times a cart carrying the sun appears in the folk traditions of Northern Europe.

The Helpful Sun

Wherever we look among the formally recorded mythologies and spiritualities of the world, we find the sun portrayed as a god or goddess. In Sumerian myth, the sun is the god Shamash, who undergoes terrible privation and torture to bring light and life to humanity. Bearded and long-armed, Shamash is often described as emerging from the doors of heaven in the East at dawn and making a daily journey across the

This relief from eighth century B.C.E. Assyria depicts the sun god Shamash setting forth on his daily journey across the heavens.

skies to enter heaven again at dusk by a parallel set of doors on the Western horizon. Cylinder seals show two gods opening the doors of heaven for Shamash to come forth. The god brandishes his emblem, a pruning saw with an arc-shaped blade and large, jagged teeth. Saws of this type are still commonly used in the Near East to this day.

Presumably because the sun sees everything in its path across the skies, Shamash came to be regarded as a god of truth, justice, and fairness. He was also a warrior—a protector of right and a destroyer of evil. It was believed that Shamash took a keen interest in the affairs of humankind. One of the early kings of Uruk was called a "son of Shamash," and the god was considered to be a protector of later kings of that city. In the great Sumerian epic of Gilgamesh, Shamash helps the mighty warrior defeat the monster Humbaba, while in a Sumerian poem "Dunluzi's Dream," he helps the hero escape from demons who have come to take him to the underworld.

Aten, the One God

In Egypt, in the period between 1379 and 1362 B.C.E., the sun ruled supreme. During that time, Pharaoh Amenhotep IV, better known as Akhenaten, proclaimed the sun, which he named Aten, to be the highest ruler of heaven. Often considered to be the first monotheist, Akhenaten did his best to subsume the rest of the original Egyptian pantheon into this single form. New temples were built in honor of Aten, a name that refers to the sun in both its physical and spiritual manifestations. As the solar cult spread through Egypt from Akhenaten's city at Heliopolis (the "City of the Sun"), every local god became identified accordingly. This sun-centered religion was the ancient world's first attempt to reduce a pantheon of deities to a single all-embracing creator god.

A hymn to Aten, probably composed by one of Akhenaten's court poets, evokes a poignant yearning for the sun's rays:

How beautiful you appear on the horizon of heaven.
O living Aten, you who were the first to live.
When you rise on the eastern horizon,
You fill every land with your beauty.

When you set on the western horizon,
There earth is in darkness, resembling death.
At daybreak, when you arise in the horizon,
Shining forth as Aten by day,
You dispel the darkness and shed your rays
Upon each and every thing.

Akhenaten's focus upon the sun as an all-embracing deity earned him the hatred of the priestly cast, especially those in service to the original sun god Ra, who was demoted in the new regime to a servant of Aten. Eventually, so powerful was the resistance to what was virtually a new religion, Akhenaten was proclaimed a heretic. After his death Akhenaten's name and deeds were deliberately expunged from the royal records and his temples torn down by the new pharaoh, who restored the old gods to their supremacy and demoted Aten to the status of a minor deity.

This relief from an Eygptian altar stone shows Akhenaten and his wife Nefertiti bathed in the rays of Aten, the sun (c. 1355 B.C.E.).

The Perfect Youth

The Greek sun god Apollo was a shining and supremely beautiful youth whose gifts to humankind were those of the spirit, including creativity, especially through music, and prophecy.

Apollo was the offspring of a liaison between Zeus and the nymph Leto. He was born on Delos, a tiny and desolate island in the Aegean, which became an important temple site and ritual center for the ancient Greeks. At his birth, which took place on the seventh day of the month, groups of swans made a circuit of the island seven times. His twin sister Artemis (or Diana, associated with the moon), who assisted in his delivery, gave a shout of joy, while Delos itself grew radiant with light. This tradition seems to echo an old belief that at the hour of sunrise, an audible cry escapes from the horizon with the first beam of light.

Zeus gifted the infant Apollo with a magical cap, a lyre, and a chariot drawn by swans. Soon after his birth the swans carried the young god off to the land of the Hyperboreans in the Far North, where for six months of the year, the climate was marked by sunshine and gentle breezes, while the Mediterranean knew the chill rains of winter.

Apollo's most significant adventure was his battle over control of the oracle at Delphi. The solitude and natural beauty of this peaceful vale in Crissa at the heart of Greece drew the god to the spot, but Hera, the mother of the gods, jealous of this latest offspring of her husband Zeus infidelities, set the great serpent Pytho in his path. A mighty combat ensued from which Apollo emerged victorious.

Some mythologists believe that Apollo's contest with the serpent signifies the war that the sun god wages with the river god in the myths of many cultures. Others believe that the battle is between an older, Mother Goddess, represented by the serpent, and the new male sky gods, represented by Apollo. In either case, Apollo was the winner, although the priestess who entered into a trance and delivered the

The temple of Apollo at Delphi, Greece, was a center of sun worship in the ancient classical world.

pronouncements of the Delphic oracle was called the Pythoness, honoring the previous tradition.

After vanquishing his adversary, Apollo cast about for worshipers. Looking seaward he is said to have beheld a Cretan ship sailing for Pylos. He turned into a dolphin, plunged into the sea, boarded the ship, and guided it to the bay of Crissa. There the god left the ship in the form of a blazing star and ascended into his temple. Now assuming the form of a handsome

left
A Tunisian mosaic portrait of the sun god
Apollo depicts a youthful boy.

below
This second-century Roman statue
shows Mithras slaying the great
Bull of the Heavens.

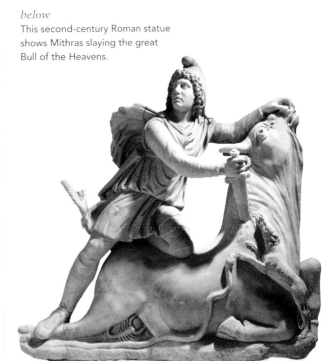

youth with wavy locks, he greeted the crew and invited them to worship him as Apollo Delphinus, a name that recalls that he first met them in the form of a dolphin. From this myth Delphi derives its name. For over a thousand years, Delphi was the center of the cult of Apollo.

In addition to music and song, Apollo brought the blessings of the harvest to the ancient Greeks. His solar nature is revealed in statues that show him with a full and flowing beard, representing the sun's rays. Generally he is given the body of a youthful athlete.

The Unconquered Sun

The story of Rome's worship of the sun is complex, blending Persian and Syrian as well as Roman beliefs. Initially the Romans had a single sun god, Sol, but subsequent influences from the variety of cultures that came under Roman rule brought them several others. When they first adopted the Greek Apollo in 433 B.C.E., he was regarded not as a god of the sun but as a god of healing and physical blessing.

Another influence came through the Syrian wife of the Emperor Septimus Severus (193–211 C.E.), who brought a taste of her own beliefs to the Roman world. Following upon this influence, the next Roman emperor, Elegabalus, considered himself to be a high priest of the Syrian sun god El-Gabal. He installed this god as part of the Roman pantheon and enforced worship of El-Gabal on Rome's citizens.

After Elegabalus was assassinated, Rome's next emperor was Aurelian, who ruled from 270–275 C.E. A devotee of the Persian sun god Mithras, he made worship of the sun in the form of Mithras central to the Roman state religion. Aurelian instituted the worship of Sol Invictus, the Unconquered Sun, heavily subsidizing the new cult and endowing it with a college of priests.

The Christian Cult of the Sun

The influence of the Roman sun cult on Christianity is beyond dispute. In 200 C.E., the theologian Clement of Alexandria described Christ as the sun driving his chariot across the sky, but the association of the sun with the Christian god was not confirmed until the reign of the Emperor Constantine, who was a devout follower of Sol Invictus. Just before he met a rival claimant for the throne in a great battle, Constantine had a vision. He saw a cross superimposed on the noonday sun and heard the words "conquer by this sign." After he won the battle, Constantine converted to Christianity and in 324 C.E. declared it the new state religion.

It seems likely that Constantine identified Christ with Sol Invictus. As a result, images of Sol, Mithras,

This seventeenth-century icon of the Enthroned Christ displays solar attributes and includes some striking similarities to the mosaic of Apollo on page 43.

and Apollo began to be integrated into Roman religious practice. The birthday of Mithras, December 25th, was adopted as the date of the nativity of Christ, and the parallels between the stories of these older gods and Christ were emphasized. Christian altars began to be oriented toward the East, as they had been in pagan sun temples. The new Christian liturgy was full of solar imagery, describing Christ as the sun, blazing a trail across the heavens and into the hearts of his followers.

Christ's mother Mary also was given solar qualities. A famous passage from Revelation, later seen as a prophetic description of the Blessed Virgin,

Not of mother nor father

was my creation.

I was made from the ninefold elements —

From fruit trees, from paradisial fruit,

From primroses and hill-flowers,

From the blossom of trees and bushes,

From the roots of the earth was I made,

From the broom and the nettle,

From the water of the ninth wave.

TRANS. CAITLÍN MATTHEWS

reads: "And there appeared a great wonder in heaven; a woman clothed with the sun, and the moon under her feet, and upon her head a crown of twelve stars." In France it is still believed that summer Saturdays are always sunny because on that day the Virgin washes the infant Jesus' shirt, which needs to be fresh and dry for Sunday!

Christ, the Risen Sun

Perceived similarities between the lives of Apollo and Christ helped shape later Christian traditions. Both were born in comparative obscurity. Because of Hera's jealousy, Leto, the mother of Apollo, sought desperately for a suitable place to bear her offspring, coming at last to a desolate island in the midst of the sea. Mary found refuge at the time of Christ's birth in a humble shelter for beasts of the field. Three gifts were presented to Apollo at his birth, the same number of gifts presented by the Magi to the infant Jesus. Further, soon after his birth, Apollo was hurried away to a peaceful land; in like manner, the child Jesus was conveyed out of danger to a place of safety.

Like Apollo, too, whose death every nightfall was ignominious, Christ's crucifixion seemed a humble end. Yet, for both, death was but a prelude to greater glory. The reappearance of the triumphant sun after its nightly death was considered by early Christians to be a prefigurement of Christ's resurrection. To them, Christ, too, was a God of Light.

This early seventeenth-century painting by Velázquez shows Apollo at the Forge of Vulcan. Note the "Christ-like" halo of golden light.

Sun Gods of North America

Native American lore is rich in stories and traditions relating to the sun and provides us with vivid accounts of sun worship. For example, the painting opposite depicts the myth of a young girl whose marvelous cloak is stolen by the sun; and the following tale, from the Thompson River people, is typical of many legends collected from native peoples of the American continent.

There was once a mischievous and incorrigible youth who wandered away from his home. When he returned, he found that his parents had deserted him. His old grandmother, who was unable to travel, was left behind. She taught the boy how to make a bow and arrows, and with these he provided a daily supply of food. She also made

The Dakota peoples referred to the sun as the "Mysterious One of the Day," and believed that he watched over them in times of need.

blankets for him out of the skins of many colored birds. These blankets were so beautiful that they attracted the attention of the Sun. It had always been the custom of the Sun to travel about naked during the day and to clothe himself only in the hours of darkness. When the Sun saw the boy's beautiful blankets, he purchased them from him, wrapped them about his body, and disappeared. Ever after, at sunset, you can see the gorgeous colors of these robes in the western sky, especially the rich blue tint of the blue jay blanket, but of the Sun nothing at all.

The Iroquois regarded the sun as a god and offered him tobacco, a practice they called "smoking the sun." On important occasions, warriors squatted in a circle while their chief lit the sacred pipe and offered it to the rising sun three times, imploring its protection and recommending the people to its care. The chief then took several puffs and passed the pipe for others to smoke in turn. As in many Christian churches today (where priests burn incense in lanterns), the prayers of the people were wafted upward by the incenselike smoke that wreathed from the sacred pipe.

Some Native Americans offered the sun the first game killed on hunting expeditions. The Apalachees of Florida, however, believed that since the sun was the source of all life, it would look with displeasure on the destruction of any creature, so they did not sacrifice animals. Instead they saluted the sun at the doors of their houses as it rose and set. In the

Native American cultures feature many vivid accounts of sun worship—the practice of smoking sacred pipes is one example.

sacred hut or cave where they worshiped, the sun's rays illuminated the altar at times of ceremonial importance, especially the solstices. In the course of worship, the Apalachees released birds sacred to the sun through a crevice in the roof of the cave temple. As they winged upward toward the sun, these birds were believed to convey the people's prayers and words of faith up to the god.

Among the native peoples of Louisiana, it was customary for the chief to face the east each morning and prostrate himself before the rising sun. He also smoked toward it, and then toward the three other cardinal points of the compass. These same people reserved a circular hut some thirty feet in diameter as a house for the sun. In it, a perpetual fire was kept burning and prayers were offered to the sun three times a day. The bones of departed chiefs were placed in this structure.

The Dakota peoples referred to the sun as the "Mysterious One of the Day" and believed that he watched over them in times of need. The following Dakota praise song, despite the clear influence of nineteenth-century Christian hymn writers, gives us a good idea of the way these people perceived the sun:

O Great Spirit, ruler of our lives,
O Great Spirit, ruler of all things visible and
   invisible,
O Great Spirit, ruler of every Spirit, good or bad,
Command the good to be favorable toward us,
And deter the bad from the practice of evil.
O Great Spirit, when hidden in the West,
Protect us from our enemies who violate the night.
Make known to us your pleasure by sending to us
   the Spirit of Dreams.
O Great Spirit, sleep no longer in the darkened West,
But return and call your people to light and life.

The Native American girl in this myth has her rainbow cloak stolen by the sun.

The Woman in the Sun

In the West, we have grown used to thinking of the sun as male and the moon as female, an idea carried over from Classical tradition. Yet in Britain until the sixteenth century, feminine pronouns were used in referring to the sun, since the word *sunne* in Old English was feminine.

In fact, a number of cultures have described the sun as feminine and seen it as containing all the beauty, warmth, and wisdom of womankind. In South Australia, the Karraru Aborigines speak of the Sun Mother, who steps across the earth every morning to bring it back to life from nightly death. Among the Norse people, the goddess Sol drives her chariot through the heavens pulled by two mighty steeds, *Aarvak* and *Alsvidir* (Early-Wake and All-Swift). She carries a shield called *Svalin* (the Cooler) and returns as night falls to her golden bed in the underworld. Her other names are *Alfrodull* (Elf Beam), or more grandly, "She who shines on the Elves."

In the Baltic region, including Latvia, Lithuania, and Prussia, the sun is worshiped as Saule, a divinity often described as the creatrix of the world. Saule divided the world into two parts: the earth, known as "vi saule," where humankind live and where the sun shines all day, and the underworld, known as "vina saule," where the dead live and where the sun goes at night. Saule is nearly always described as metallic and shining. She spins precious metals and dresses in dazzling silks embroidered with gold, silver, and bronze. On Midsummer morning, she is said to dance in silver shoes, and her most often used symbols— wheels, rings, circled crosses, and crosses casting out golden rays—reflect movement and light.

This stunning Australian Aborigine painting called "Women's Ceremony" places the sun at the very center of a dramatic earthy red world.

In the same region the sun is portrayed as a red apple falling from a tree into the ocean. At sunset, the tears of the goddess turn into red berries, explaining the red sky. An old song from the Baltic countries says:

The Sun in the golden garden
Weeps bitterly;
The golden apple
Has fallen from the tree.

In cultures where the sun in female, the moon is often male. With the feminine associated with day rather than night the sun is also the bringer of health, vitality, and the practical skills of daily living, as the tale overleaf from Central and Eastern Europe shows.

The Woman in the Sun

This Slavic tale tells how a man finds welcome and renewal in the house of the sun. The feminine sun brings new life to those who are weary and worn, whether from the day's work or from a long life.

The House at the End of the World

Once a man came to the end of the world and looked around. He was very tired because he had walked from the beginning of the world, and his food had run out long ago. There before him he saw a red house with curtains at the windows and smoke making a lazy trail in the sky. With hope in his heart, he knocked at the door. After a moment an old woman in black opened the door.

"Please," said the man, "I have walked from the beginning of the world. Please may I come inside and rest?"

The old woman looked at him for a moment; then she invited him in, taking his arm and guiding him to sit down before a simple wooden table. She brought him hot water and a towel and bade him wash.

"My daughter will be home soon," she said. "Then we will eat."

Moments later a girl in a bright scarlet dress entered the room. Her face shone with light, and her smile lit up the whole house. When the man looked at her, he felt warmth well up inside him, as though he were young again.

"My dear," said the old woman, "we have a guest. This wanderer has walked from the beginning of the world."

"What a lot you must have seen," said the girl, her voice sounding like honey drops falling from a spoon.

They ate in silence, for the man was suddenly shy and could think of nothing to say, not even about his long journey. In the warmth of the house, with a full stomach, he began to grow sleepy.

Seeing this, the old woman showed him to a bed in the corner, piled high with skins. He lay down at once, but as he was drifting off to sleep, he saw the girl take off her scarlet dress and lie down in another part of the room. Her mother took the dress, which seemed to shine with a light of its own, and hung it up beside the fireplace. Then she took a piece of black cloth and covered it up. At once, the room grew dark, and the man fell into a deep sleep.

Just before dawn, he woke to hear the old woman singing a quiet song to the girl, gently chiding her: "Come, my Solntse, my little sun. The night is growing old. Get up and go about your work."

At once, the girl rose and put on her dress. Suddenly light filled the room. Then, so swiftly he was scarcely aware of it, the man felt warm lips brush his cheek, and the girl was gone. For a moment, the man thought he saw shining wings unfolding from her back, but afterward he could never be sure whether that vision was just part of a dream.

But ever after, the man spoke of the girl at the end of the world in hushed tones, and sometimes, he would look up at the sun riding high across the heavens and smile and wave as though to an old friend.

Heroes of the Sun

The sun also had heroes: extraordinary, powerful beings who brought their own light to the world. The nature of these beings helped define the qualities of the summer season, as well as the heavenly orb itself. These heroes, in turn, were defined by the sun's qualities and are thus frequently portrayed as hotheaded, swift footed, fiery, aggressive, and hugely energetic.

In Irish myth, for example, we read of the hero Cuchulainn, whose strength grew greater toward the middle of the day and waned with the sun's passing. Before a battle, madness would come upon him. Afterward Cuchulainn had to be dunked in a bath of cold water to cool him down.

Similar stories are recorded of the Arthurian hero Gawain of Orkney, whose strength also waxed and waned with the sun. This heroic knight dressed in red and wore a golden five-pointed star on his breast. Celtic myth is full of thinly disguised sun heroes. Some have names that give them away, like Gwri Golden Hair; others, like Lug or Llew, are radiant beings who carry spears or swords of light.

Among the Norse people, Balder combines heroic and godlike qualities. Radiantly beautiful, Balder is described as having rays of light shining from his body. He was the sweetest spoken of the *Aesir* (High Gods) and also the most fair minded. He lived in a part of heaven called *Breidablik* (Broad Gleam), where nothing unclean or accursed could dwell.

The same godlike qualities are given to the Greek hero Hercules, who began life as the half-immortal son of Zeus but was gradually transformed through his extraordinary deeds into a god. That Hercules is a child of the sun is clear, because he is often described as glowing eyed, golden, and fiery. His twelve famous labors mark him as a calendar deity, one of those heroes who, like Gilgamesh in Sumerian mythology, undertakes a series of adventures over the course of a year, each of which can be seen to signify one of the months.

In later times, after Europe had been converted to Christianity, these and other godlike solar heroes were reduced to shadowy beings, behind whom we can still catch glimpses of their mightier forebears. The original solar heroes appear most clearly in the festival observances of the ritual year, and in this book, we meet them again and again. Thus figures like the Lord and Lady of Summer, found all over Europe, reigned over the celebration of the Midsummer Solstice hundreds of years after their greater forms had become antiquarian curiosities.

above
Gawain, the solar hero of Arthurian romance, faces the Green Knight in this illustration from a fourteenth-century poem.

right
A fresco from the House of Pompeii, Italy, showing the infant Hercules wrestling with snakes.

The Lost Sun

Some solar heroes must rescue the sun when it gets lost. This story from the Baltic may be one of the oldest versions of this tale. It was recorded in a life of St. Jerome, who visited the area in 1431 and found the people worshiping a giant hammer. In this story we learn why. As recently as 1928, this story was still being told in Lithuania during the festival of Midsummer.

The Sun, the Stars, and the Hammer

Long ago—so long that no one remembers when—Saule the sun became trapped in a great tower at the edge of the world. How she came to be there is a mystery. Some say she wandered into the tower out of curiosity and was trapped when the wind slammed the door. Others say she was stolen away and shut up there by some jealous god. In either case, there she was and there she stayed, while on the earth, all was in darkness.

In time the cries of the people reached the ears of the Constellations. They circled the world, listening and looking for ways to help set the sun free. Finally they went to Kalvaitis, the Smith of Heaven.

"Please Kalvaitis," they said, "we have come to ask you to make a great hammer."

"Why should I do that?" demanded the Smith God. "I have plenty of hammers."

"You must do it," chorused the Constellations, "because Saule has been locked in a tower and cannot get out. A hammer made by you is the only thing strong enough to break down the tower."

When he heard this, Kalvaitis hesitated. He had many things to do. But the Constellations gathered about him, offering words of encouragement, each promising to lend him their strength, wit, wisdom, or cleverness to aid his work.

Finally Kalvaitis agreed and set to work. For five days and nights he labored, and all the while the Constellations sang to him and gave him their energies.

At last, when the hammer was done, the Smith God took it in his mighty hands and strode to the edge of the world where the tower stood. All was in darkness save a few gleams of bright golden light spilling out from cracks in the stone.

"Are you there, Saule?" called Kalvaitis.

Faintly he heard the voice of the Sun calling back. She seemed to be weeping. Kalvaitis swung the hammer. One, twice, three times, he struck the tower. Then with a great crash, it burst apart and Saule leaped free. The sun shone out over the world again, and everywhere people rejoiced.

Ever after, it is said, Saule had a special kindness for the smith, but even more she loved the Constellations, without whose help she might never have been set free.

The smith is one of the most powerful figures in Western mythology and very much a solar hero. As figures of unearthly strength and creators, smiths were regarded in many cultures as powerful beings. This story seems designed to explain the weakening of the sun at Midwinter and its return to splendor at Midsummer. Here it is the Constellations who aid in Saule's release, but in earlier days people offered sacrifices to help call back the sun.

In the figures of the male solar hero and the feminine sun, we see prototypes of characters who appear in later folklore traditions. The following chapters take us into that later world, in which the gods and heroes of the sun appear in different guises, but the games and celebrations of the solstice continue unabated.

Journey to the Sun: A Meditation

Though we may no longer regard the sun as a divinity as our ancestors did, the sun can still be a very important personal symbol for us, its light every bit as vital as it was in the cosmos of our ancestors. In the meditation that follows, you may take a journey of your own, following in the steps of the solar heroes/heroines about whom you have just been reading.

The first part of the journey is conducted through guided imagery, but later you will be asked to use your own inner senses to explore the mystery of the sun's course through your life. When you reach that point in the journey, follow the way you are led, either by your own inner compass or by the helpers who are everywhere present. It may be an inner sun that you seek, a light that no longer shines as it once did for you. Or, you may track the influence of the real sun on your life. By making your own pilgrimage in search of the sun, you are sure to arrive at a deeper understanding of its energies.

When you stand before the Lord and Lady of Midsummer, you are meeting the most human appearances of the sun gods and goddesses of antiquity. From them, you can learn much about the state of your personal sun.

❧ *Close your eyes and allow your outer senses to switch off. Prepare to leave behind your everyday consciousness and to travel into another reality. Then, with your inner senses, become aware of a mighty tree rising before you. Its trunk is the span of a dozen trees; its branches wide and thick. It is easy to climb, and this you do, climbing up and up until you arrive at a place above the clouds. The light there is dim, like that just before dawn, but you are able to see a great stretch of whiteness on all sides, a landscape seemingly made of cloud. You find that you can easily walk upon this surface as if it were firm ground.*

❧ *Not knowing which way to go, you look around for directions. You see coming toward you a tall figure wrapped in a cloak of iridescent darkness. He has shining black hair and a thick beard, and his eyes gleam with a tricksterlike twinkle. This figure bids you welcome and asks why you have come.*

You answer that you have come to seek the Midsummer Sun. At this he laughs.

"Do you truly think the sun will not return without your efforts?"

Then, noting your crestfallen look, he says, "If you truly wish to seek the sun, you must travel to the home of the Lord and Lady of Midsummer. Do you wish to do this?"

❧ *You answer that you do, and your guide turns and utters a high, ululating call. At once the clouds part, and a chariot drawn by two great black steeds appears. Your guide bids you to get in, and this you do, settling back amid heaps of cushions and blankets. Your guide leaps into the driving seat, and* uttering another cry, urges the horses into motion. At once you are moving smoothly and quickly, as the white cloudscape over which you travel passes in a blur. You cannot tell how long the journey takes, or how far you have traveled, but it seems only a moment later that the chariot comes to a halt, and your guide invites you to get down. Looking around, you find yourself standing at the foot of a flight of marble stairs that rise out of the clouds and vanish into a mist shot through with a golden glow. Your guide indicates that you should proceed. You set out at once, on your own this time, but climbing upward without any fear... (Pause)

☙ After a time that is no time, you arrive at the top of the steps and find before you a long hallway that seems formed of cloud. Gentle golden light shines out on all sides, though its source is hidden. You begin to walk and soon see ahead two mighty thrones, on which are seated figures twice as tall as you. As you stand before them, you see they are a man and a woman, clad in golden robes, with crowns of gold on their brows and hair like streams of frozen light. Their eyes are azure, fathomless as the deepest sea.

As you stand before them, the Lord and Lady of Midsummer look down at you, not unkindly, and ask, in one voice, why you have come.

You tell them that you have come to find the Midsummer Sun and bring it back to shine upon the earth once more.

At this the Lady of Midsummer smiles at her Lord, who nods to her. Then the Lady addresses you. "Before you can undertake this task, you must first look into my mirror." She indicates a place off to the left, where the clouds part to reveal a shining mirror set into the shifting walls.

In your own time, you move to the place and look into the mirror. No one but you knows what you see there, but it is something important to you and to your quest ... (Pause)

☙ When you have finished looking into the mirror, the Lord of Midsummer rises from his throne and offers a blessing:

Go, with the strength
  of the summer,
with the speed of wind,
with the force of rain,
with the light of the Midsummer Sun you seek.

With these words ringing in your ears you turn away from the Lord and Lady. Behind you waits your tall dark guide; he beckons you back toward the chariot and his two black steeds—the magical chariot is ready. As you step into it, he stands back and indicates that you must continue your journey without him. The chariot will take you where you need to go, and you must trust to its knowledge.

As you settle yourself in place again, suddenly with a flurry of wings and a loud cry, a large Raven arrives. It perches on the front of the chariot and cocks its head at you. Its yellow eyes are full of mischief and wisdom. Almost at once the chariot begins to move, traveling faster and faster through the white fields of cloud. You are vaguely aware of land passing beneath; continents and oceans seem small and insignificant as you sail through the clouds. As you travel, you hear the voice of the Raven, and mingled with its words are strains of music, high and mysterious, coupled with the songs of birds. Listening, you are carried onward toward your goal...

Trust whatever you see there or look to the Raven for advice...When you arrive at the place of the Midsummer Sun, ask it to return with you, to brighten and warm your days.

With your task accomplished, return slowly to the place from which you began, allowing your inner senses to recede and your outer senses to return to normal waking consciousness. You may wish to make notes on what you saw and heard, keeping in mind that from this point forward, you journey with the blessing of the Lord of Midsummer.

A Midsummer Blessing at Stonehenge

Though the thin rain lash the broad plain
And the sword-blade's rimmed with mist,
Shake the bright light from the short night
Kiss the hele-stone in ancient tryst.

Though the long tracks know no glad step
And the circle go unblessed;
From their long homes may the old ones
Welcome travelers upon their quest.

Though the keepers greet no reapers,
And the grasses grow high;
May the Corn King dance his crop sign
In the barley, wheat, and rye.

Though remembrance be a semblance
And the land thrums with wrong,
May the hele-stone be the leal throne
Where the sun awakens song.

Chorus:
Sun-stone's kiss, Midsummer's pleasure,
Welcome all and some.
At the hele-stone sing and gather,
Every blessèd one.

CAITLÍN MATTHEWS

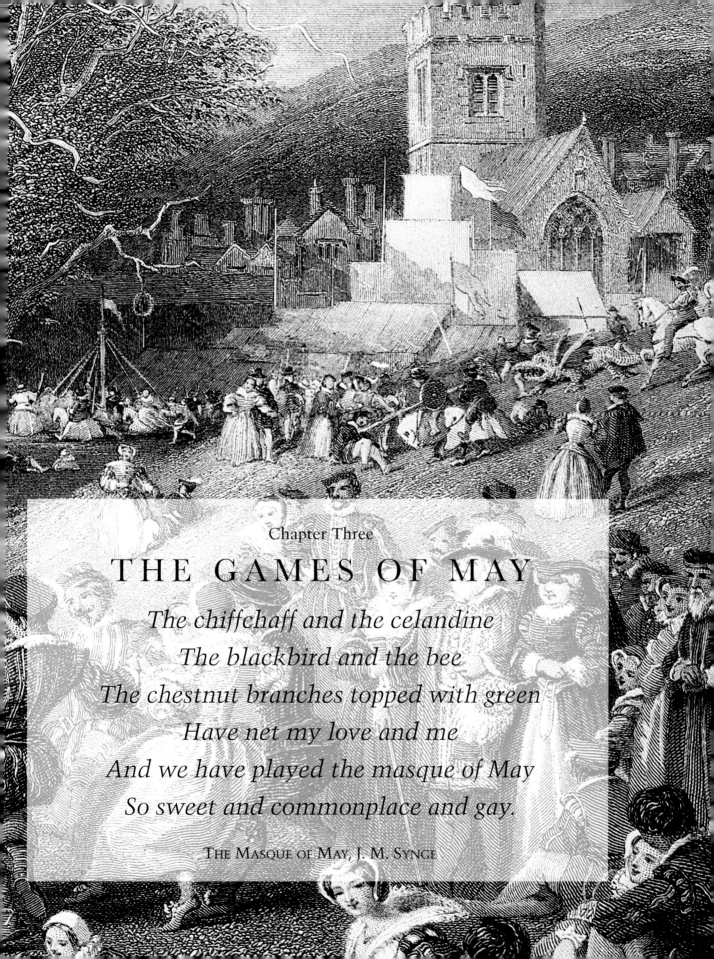

Chapter Three

THE GAMES OF MAY

The chiffchaff and the celandine
The blackbird and the bee
The chestnut branches topped with green
Have net my love and me
And we have played the masque of May
So sweet and commonplace and gay.

The Masque of May, J. M. Synge

Beltaine Fires

The sun's journey across the skies from May to September has traditionally been lit by fires, guided by signs and portents, surrounded by wonders. It is a period when dreams begun in the spring are brought to fruition, when every farmer's attention is focused on field and byre, hearth and home; when the skies are watched carefully for the secrets that might unfold through the movement of sun, moon, and stars. During this time blessings are sought and gods and spirits invoked.

May begins it all, with its passionate outpouring of wildness and abandonment, its joyful celebration of the end of winter's hold over the earth. Again, fire is a central part of the festivities. Throughout the Celtic world, the practice of lighting fires, often on hills, on the eve of May Day goes back as far as anyone can remember. The festival was originally known as Beltane or *Beiltainn*, a name probably derived from the Gaelic *tein-eigin*, "needfire," and *Beil*, a corruption of *Belenus*, a god whose worship was widespread throughout Britain and Gaul. Belenus may have been a solar god, as his name can be translated as "bright fire." The sacred fires were aimed at stimulating the sun at the beginning of the summer season, the second division of the Celtic year.

Before daylight dawned on the first of May, burning brands were carried from these fires into the houses to ignite the hearth fires that would burn continuously until the festival of Samhain on November 1. Until the end of the nineteenth century in the highlands of Scotland, Beltaine was the only occasion when the peat fires that warmed the house were put out and relighted, an echo of the Roman tradition in which the sacred fires in the temple of Vesta were doused and ceremonially ignited again on the first of March by the Vestal Virgins.

Many Beltaine fire customs have older roots. The burning of the skull or bones of a horse in a communal Beltaine fire may be a version of a sacrifice that took place at an even more ancient festival, while scattering the fire's embers on the fields to produce good crops clearly derives from ancient fertility rites. Another Beltaine custom with venerable origins is for people to dance around the fire sunwise and then run around the fields holding burning brands to stimulate the soil and the crops, as well as to drive away evil influences.

Other echoes of ancient sacrificial rites have come down to us in the form of Beltaine cakes, large round cakes of oatmeal that were rolled downhill or through the fields in some areas. At the end of the proceedings the cake was divided among the company. The person who received a piece that had been earlier marked with charcoal was known as the *cailleac-beal-teine*, the "Beltaine hag." This unfortunate person was made to leap over the fire three times, or sometimes laid on the ground to undergo a mock quartering as a

The sacred fires were aimed at stimulating the sun at the beginning of the summer season.

A great May Day bonfire commemorates the end of winter and invites the sun, on Calton Hill, Edinburgh, Scotland.

sacrificial victim. Afterward he or she was pelted with eggshells and was for a time spoken of as one who was dead. In parts of Scotland still today, a Beltaine bannock (biscuit) is cooked and broken into equal parts, one of which is smeared with ash until it is black. The parts are placed in a bag and everyone draws one. The person who gets the blackened piece has to jump around a bonfire in token of a sacrifice.

May Day Revels

The ancient roots of May Day celebrations in Northern Europe can be traced back at least as far as Roman times, though some of the customs, as we shall see, are certainly older still. One of the earliest accounts of a festival in Britain with striking similarities to the revels of May is found in the *Historia Regum Britanniae* of Geoffrey of Monmouth, a Latin pseudohistory dating from about 1130 C.E. Geoffrey's account is of a religious festival celebrating the Celtic King Cassivelaunus' defeat by Julius Caesar in circa 53 C.E.

All the barons of Britain and their wives were summoned to London to make offerings to their gods. They accordingly all came without tarrying and made sacrifice of divers kinds, and profuse slaying of cattle. Forty-thousand kine did they offer, a hundred thousand sheep, and all manner fowl at a number not lightly to be reckoned, besides thirty thousand in all

This sixteenth-century painting from the Salon of the Muses in Villa Medici, Florence, depicts a Roman feast in honor of the Gods.

of every sort of forest deer. And when they had paid all due honor unto the gods, they feasted them on the remainder...and the day and the night they spent in playing games of divers kinds.

A Saxon priest named Layamon, in his *Brut*, or *Chronicle of Britain*, elaborates this description somewhat, adding details of the sacred rites that were the centerpiece of such festivities:

The King began the rite after the heathen laws of the time. There were ten thousand men in the temple, the best of all Britons, standing before the mighty idol of Apollin [Apollo]. Each man held a torch, and each was clothed in gold, while the king wore a crown on his head. In front of the altar was a great fire set, and into this the King and all his greatest men cast gifts...Thereafter they feasted on twelve thousand oxen, three thousand harts, three thousand hinds and countless fowl...Then all the company repaired to the fields nearby, where they began to ride, and to run, and to play, while others fought with spear and shield, cast great stones, or played games on the table-board.

Both of these accounts were written down by Christian scribes, long after the event, but each has an air of authenticity that implies that the writers drew on existing documents and oral memory. There is little doubt that the revels they described were celebrations of the Celtic god Belenus, whom the Romans confused with Apollo, and who was, as we have seen, a central figure of the Beltaine festival.

In the writings of the Greek historian Diodorus Siculus, we find a description of a ceremony held at a great circle of stones in the island of the Hyperboreans, which was, from the Greek perspective, located in the far north. There Apollo was said to make an

Come lasses and lads,
Take leave of your dads,
And away to the Maypole hie;
For every he has got him a she
With a minstrel standing by:
For Willy has gotten his Jill,
And Jonny has got his Jone,
To jig it, jig it, jig it, jig it,
Jig it up and down.

ANON.

appearance every nineteen years, and there also was to be found "a city sacred to the same god, most of the inhabitants of which are harpists who continually play upon their harps in the temple and sing hymns to the God extolling his actions." Another classical writer, the Roman poet Pindar, added in his Tenth Pythian Ode:

In the banquets and praises of that people Apollo chiefly rejoiceth, and he laugheth and he looketh on the brute beasts in their ramping lewdness. Yet such are their ways that the Music is not banished, but on every side the dances of maidens and the sounds of the lyre and the notes of the flute are ever circling; and with their hair crowned with golden bay leaves they hold glad revelry.

It has long been recognized that these and other classical descriptions refer to Britain. Certainly the celebrations depicted are remarkably similar to the May Day revels, while the circle of stones in which the god appears may well be Stonehenge.

The First Day of Summer

Virtually all these ancient practices were connected in some way to the turning of the agricultural year. In Northern Europe, May Day was acknowledged as the first day of summer. The rituals of invoking the sun and the energy of summer on the first of May were critically important as they might dictate the way the whole summer season turned out. A successful growing season was essential to a successful harvest and thus to a warm, wellfed, and comfortable winter. Thus the rituals around May Day were also a means of protecting family and home during a crucial time.

In addition to its ritual observances, May Day brought changes to the patterns of daily life. Cattle that had been stall-fed through the winter and spring were turned out to pasture; sheep were moved from home fields onto rougher land. The work of tilling the soil in preparation for spring planting had been completed by this time, and signs and portents gleaned from the weather were a daily consideration. The location in the sky of the sun and moon, the strength and direction of the wind, the amount of rain, the temperature, and so forth were studied carefully for the effect they might have on the planting of grain. Folk sayings that have survived in Britain and Ireland testify to the importance of these observances:

A wet and windy May,
Fills the barns with corn and hay.

Throughout Ireland, May Day was traditionally a time to bring in large quantities of flowers, especially those with white or yellow blossoms, and decorate the house to celebrate the dawning of summer. May boughs, cut from certain trees, were laid across doorsteps and windowsills or on the roofs of the house and cow barn. In some places, these boughs were replanted in the earth around the fields and farmyards, as a protection against ill luck or evil influences.

Certain trees were considered especially lucky, such as the mountain ash, elder, broom, and hazel. The great sixteenth-century antiquary, Camdem, in his *Britannia*, remarks on this belief, noting that "upon the calends or first day of May, [the people] fully believe that to set a green bough of a tree before their houses will cause them to have great abundance of milk all summer long." Sometimes this practice was carried out more elaborately, a whole bush being uprooted and replanted close to the house or field, or at a crossroads, or on the village green. Often these bushes were decorated with bright scraps of material, or garlands of eggshells (sometimes saved from the Easter celebration), and surrounded by tallow dips or scraps of candle saved for this purpose. The landscape of rural Ireland and Britain must have looked magical on May Eve, with tiny flickering lights scattered across the country-side like fallen stars.

May Eve was a magical time when fairies came out to play, secret messages were passed between courting couples, and the landscape flickered with tiny lights.

branch of lime might equal "prime"; pear, "fair"; thorn, "scorn"; holly, "folly"; nut, "slut"; gorse, "whore(s)"; and so on. This practice may be a distant echo of the magical Ogham alphabet developed by the Celtic Bards to pass on messages, in which certain trees were associated with letters, days, or symbols that could be carved in stone.

Girls seeking husbands, or those wishing to enhance their beauty, had their own May Day ritual. They were advised to bathe in dew collected on May Day morning, the dew from the hawthorn being particularly effective, as the old verse says:

The fair maid who on the First of May
Goes to the fields at break of day
And washes in dew from the hawthorn tree
Will ever after handsome be.

May Day Visions

Though Midsummer's Night is traditionally the time when the fairy folk are abroad, they made unexpected appearances on May Day as well. It was believed that fairies could lead mortals astray, confusing them with strange lights or music, but they could as easily blight a farmer's fields or disease his cattle. On May Day, too, it was believed, fairies might steal human children and replace them with changelings. Yet a child born on May Day was believed to be lucky and to have the ability to see the fairies.

Some May Day customs seem to be based on people's fear of fairy folk. The noise and commotion people made at May Day celebrations was aimed at scaring away the fairies. Farther back in time, noisemaking may have been an aspect of a ceremony in which an animal or human sacrifice was made to propitiate the older nature gods (who, in fact, became the fairies in later times).

This same custom was put to a very different use in the tradition of "May Birching," which was widely practiced in the eastern and southern parts of Britain until recently. Here, on May Eve people crept through darkened villages and hung branches outside the houses of those to whom they wished to pass a particular message. The message was passed in a kind of code, the meaning carried by words that rhymed with the names of particular bushes. Thus a

May Day myths, poems, and folk stories include many spirit and fairy elements—this is *Night with her Train of Stars* by Edward Hughes.

It was also believed that the gates between the worlds opened for a brief time on May Eve to let the shades of the dead walk abroad. At Loch Aishie, just south of Inverness in Scotland, people used to say that two phantom armies, believed to be the dead who fell in a battle won by the great Irish hero Fionn mac Cumhail, can still be seen fighting on May Day morning. Farther south, in Cambridgeshire, England, fishermen refused to take their boats out to sea on May Day, since they feared they would see the dead floating under the surface of the water. Seeing a ghost on May Day could be either lucky or unlucky, depending on the notoriously capricious nature of the spirit in question.

Many May Day stories include supernatural elements. A wonderful fourteenth-century English poem, "Sir Orfeo," adapts the Greek myth of Orpheus and Euridyce for a courtly audience. According to the poem, on May Day, Queen Heurodis falls asleep beneath an apple tree and dreams of the Fairy King. He shows her the delights of his realm

and promises to come for her that very night. When Heurodis tells her husband King Orfeo about the dream, he set guards around her. Nevertheless, in the morning, she has vanished away.

Distraught, Orfeo gives his lands into the keeping of a trusted regent and, taking only his harp, sets off wandering the world in search of his love, growing ever wilder and more deranged. At last, after ten years, as he lies by the side of stream, Orfeo spies the fairy court riding by. Among them is Heurodis. Orfeo follows and manages to enter the fairy kingdom through a crack in some rocks.

He wins an audience with the Fairy King and overwhelms the court with the beauty of his harp playing. So moved is the king by Orfeo's music that he offers Orfeo any gift he chooses. Orfeo asks for his beloved Heurodis. Though the Fairy King hesitates, he concedes, and the two mortals are allowed to leave. Happily re-united, Orfeo and Heurodis return home to rule over their kingdom.

Another tale tells of Taliesin, the great shaman-bard of the Celts, who is found as a baby in a leather bag drifting in a boat on May Eve by the unlucky Prince Elfin. On opening the bag, Elfin sees a bright light shining from the baby's forehead. "Behold, a radiant brow!" he cries. "Tal-iesin "radiant brow" in Welsh] shall I be called," replies the precocious child and goes on to sing the first of many extraordinary poems:

Fair Elfin, cease your sorrow!
Cursing profits no one.
It is not evil to hope,
Nor does any man see what supports him.
No catch in Gwyddno's weir
Was ever as good as tonight's.

From this time Elfin's ill luck changed, while Taliesin went on to become the greatest poet in ancient Britain and King Arthur's own bard.

Pagan Pastimes

The gradual spread of Christianity throughout the West caused the older beliefs surrounding May Day to go underground. That they did not die testifies to the strength of these beliefs and to the determination of ordinary men and women to keep them alive.

When Christianity was declared the state religion by the Emperor Constantine in the fourth century, many beliefs and practices of the "old religion" were appropriated by the newly established Church and adapted as "Christian," as happened with the mysteries of Mithras and Apollo. The great festivals of the seasons, such as the solstice celebrations we looked at in chapter one, were taken over and used as the basis for a Christian calendar of holy days dedicated to the saints and apostles.

But many people, who remembered the original significance of the solstices and other seasonal observances, continued the older practices in secret behind closed doors. With the passage of time, the ancient ways became entwined with folk traditions, or what were called "country beliefs," and attached themselves to more official (and thus more Christian) celebrations. Though Church officials may have thought that they had stamped out such "pagan" practices, the folk were not so easily bullied. They simply changed the names of the characters in their old stories to Christian ones, or drew the newcoming saints and heroes of Christianity into their traditional seasonal celebrations. It is important to remember, after all, that the real meaning of the term *pagan* is "a rustic; someone from the country."

Bacchus, the Roman god of food and wine, was slowly forgotten when Christianity became the state religion; Caravaggio's portrait shows a world-weary face.

Attacks by the Church

The abundant descriptions of games, sports, fairs, dances, and races held between May Day and Midsummer make it clear that annual fairs, all probably derived from ancient solstice worship, were firmly established as early as the thirteenth century. That these country celebrations were regarded as dangerously pagan is made clear by the number of attacks mounted against them by the Church. In a sermon delivered before King Edward VI in 1549, Bishop Latimer describes how he came to a place on his way back to London where it had been announced that he intended to preach on a Sunday morning:

Because it was a holy day, and me thought it was a holy day's work; the church stood in my way; and I took my horse and my company and went thither; I thought I should have found a great company in the church, and when I came there the church door was fast locked. I tarried there half an hour and more, and at last the key was found; and one of the parish comes to me, and says: "Sir, this is a busy day with us, we cannot hear you; it is Robin Hood's Day. The parish are gone abroad to gather for Robin Hood." I thought my rochet [red robe] would have been regarded, though I were not; but it would not serve; it was fain to give way to Robin Hood's men.

Though we may smile at this picture of the outraged bishop, languishing outside a locked church while his parishioners are off gathering for Robin Hood, this incident offers a clear indication of how important the May games were to the people of medieval England.

Nor did things alter much in succeeding centuries. In 1736, the minister of the deanery of Stowe in Gloucestershire issued a tract aimed against the celebration of May Day games, which he called evident "relics of paganism" and no more than thinly disguised echoes of "sacrificial worship."

What exactly was it that took place at the May Day games that so alarmed and angered the Church? Accounts differ, but it is possible to find a pattern in the descriptions that gives us insight into the hidden significance of these celebrations.

The Pole of the Heavens

The most important of the May Day rituals was bringing in and raising the Maypole. Throughout most of Europe, a new pole, most often oak, elm, or birch, was brought from the forest each May and erected in

> The most important of the May Day rituals was bringing in and raising the Maypole.

Robin Hood was a central figure in English May Day festivities. Here he is played by Errol Flynn in the 1938 film, *The Adventures of Robin Hood.*

At Scuttlebrooke Wake, Chipping
Campden, U.K., the Beltaine celebrations
echo those of ages past.

the town or village square, where it became the focus of joyful and uninhibited games, feasting, and merriment.

The origin of this custom dates back at least as far as classical times, when a Phrygian pine tree, sacred to the Roman god Attis, was taken in procession to the temple of his consort, the Mother Goddess Cybele. Attis was the god of cattle, sheep, and plants. His death (or castration) just after the spring equinox was preceded by a vigil of fasting and abstinence, from which was derived the Christian observance of Lent. Then, after a night in the grave, Attis was resurrected, and mourning turned to delight and rejoicing. Priests of Cybele danced through the streets clothed in motley garments that foreshadow the beribboned dancers of medieval Europe. The Roman festival celebrating Attis' resurrection was known as the *Hilaria*, the "Festival of Joy." Among its customs,

strands of wool were tied to the top of the sacred pine tree, and dancers revolved ecstatically around it. The essence of this festival was brought to Europe by the Roman legions and remained after they left, transforming itself over the years into something like the current celebration of May Day.

There are many accounts of traditional Maypole dancing and the joyful celebrations that accompanied it. In Wales, according to folklorist Marie Trevelyan:

On the morning of May Day—that is, at the very first glimmer of dawn—youths and maidens in nearly every parish in Wales set out to the nearest woodlands. The gay procession consisted of men with horns and other instruments, which were played, while vocalists sang the songs of May time. When the merry party reached the woodlands, each member broke a bough off a tree, and decorated the branch with flowers, unless they were already laden with May blossoms. A tall birch tree was cut down and born on a farm wagon drawn by oxen into the village. At sunrise the young people placed the branches of May beside the doors or in the windows of their houses.

This was followed by the setting up of the Maypole on the village green. The pole was decorated with nosegays and garlands of flowers, interspersed with brightly colored ribbon bows, rosettes, and streamers. Then the master of ceremonies, or leader of the May dancers, would advance to the pole, and tie a gay-colored ribbon around it. He was followed by all the dancers, each one approaching the pole and tying a ribbon around it until a certain number had been tied. The dance then began, each dancer taking his or her place according to the order in which the ribbons had been arranged around the pole. The dance was continued without intermission until the party was tired, and then other dancers took their places.

Children in New Haven, Connecticut, show that the May Day traditions transferred easily to the New World.

This custom has many levels of meaning. The connection of the Maypole to ancient fertility rites is clear. The erect pole is clearly phallic, symbolic of the planting of seeds in Mother Earth. This association accounts for the frequent attempts by the Church (especially the Puritans of the sixteenth century) to suppress the celebration of May Day as a remnant of pagan superstition. But the Maypole was far more than this.

In the mythologies of many cultures, from Siberia to Mesoamerica, Africa to the Mediterranean, the world is supported by a cosmic tree, a central axis that links earth and heaven and has existed since creation. Plato placed the pole at the center of his model of the Cosmos, giving it the name "The Spindle of Necessity," and giving it into the care of the goddess Anake, whose name means necessity. Along with her daughters, the Moirai or Fates, Anake spins the destiny of the world from a point somewhere out in the Milky Way.

Thus the dance around the Maypole may be, at its deepest level, an acknowledgment of humanity's place in the cosmos, its fate intertwined like ribbons with the circling rounds of the sun, the stars, the seasons, and other natural forces. Through the dance, the people wound themselves into the very heart of creation, echoing cyclical patterns that had existed since the beginning of time. Maypole celebrations emphasized the human desire for earthly joy and brought the essence of the natural world into the domestic circle of home and community. As the poet R. L. Stevenson put it in his "Twelve Months":

Why should the priest against the May-pole preach?
Alas! it is a thing out of his reach;
How he the error of the time condoles,

And says, 'tis none of the celestial poles;
Whilst he (fond man!) at May-poles thus perplext,
Forgets he makes a May-game of his text.
But May shall triumph at a higher rate,
Having trees for poles, and boughs to celebrate;
And the green regiment, in brave array,
Like Kent's great waling grove, shall bring in May.

The King and Queen of May

The central figures in many May Day celebrations were the King and Queen of the May, who reigned over the joyous welcoming of the summer. Various suggestions have been put forward as to their origin. Some see the Queen as a representation of the Roman goddess Flora, the deity of spring, and the King as a later aspect of another primordial figure, the Green Man, representative of the male principle in nature. Another explanation identifies the Queen of the May with Cybele, the Roman Mother Goddess whose son-consort Attis is resurrected each spring.

But the May Queen is older by far than Roman times. In fact, no one can say with certainty where she and her consort originated. It seems most likely that they derive from ancient representations of the season itself, possibly once represented by sacred effigies carried in procession, or in flower-bedecked ox carts similar to the sun carts described in chapter one, which were pulled through towns and villages and then displayed in a sacred grove or stone circle.

Mythologically, the May Queen is a type of Flower Bride, the consort of the Earth God himself, and she appears under a variety of names and forms. An echo of her original nature may be seen in the Welsh figure *Blodeuwedd* (Flower Face), who was created from flowers and fruits by the magician gods Math and Gwydion. The following poem, attributed to the bard Taliesin, describes the May Queen as incorporating the elements of the earth and the attributes of the spring and summer seasons.

Not of mother nor father was my creation.
I was made from the ninefold elements—
From fruit trees, from paradisial fruit,
From primroses and hill-flowers,
From the blossom of trees and bushes,
From the roots of the earth was I made,
From the broom and the nettle,
From the water of the ninth wave...
(translation by Caitlín Matthews)

At some point, the effigies carried in the ritual gave way to brightly garbed human beings who stood as physical representations of the deities. Throughout the Middle Ages, these ancient figures can be recognized in the white-clad, golden-crowned maiden and her lusty, green-clad lord who stand at the center of the revels, often under the names of Robin Hood and Maid Marian from the stories of the great British folk hero and his love.

The elegant birch tree recalls the decorated Maypole seen everywhere at this time of year.

The Struggle for the Maiden of Spring

A deeper theme yet lies behind the figure of the May Queen. At one time, as the Maiden of Spring, she was the focus of a cosmic battle between the Gods of Summer and Winter. The month of May, perceived as a boundary time that divides winter and summer, became the arena in which an age-old struggle for control of the season was enacted. We catch sight of this ancient conflict in an episode from the medieval Welsh story "Culhwch and Olwen."

Creiddylad, the daughter of Lludd Llaw Ereint, and Gwythyr, the son of Greidawl, were betrothed. And before she had become his bride, Gwynn ap Nudd came and carried her away by force; and Gwythyr, the son of Greidawl, gathered his host together, and went to fight with Gwynn ap Nudd. But Gwynn overcame him...When Arthur heard of this, he went to the North, and summoned Gwynn ap Nudd before him...and made peace between...[him]...and Gwythyr the son of Greidawl. And this was the peace that was made: that the maiden should remain in her father's house, without advantage to either of them, and that Gwynn ap Nudd and Gwythyr son of Greidawl should fight for her every first of May, from thenceforth until the day of doom, and that whichever of them should then be conqueror should have the maiden.

Clearly, the reason that there can be no overall winner of the maiden until "the day of doom" when the world ends is because the two adversaries stand for winter and summer, the seasonal energies that struggle each May for possession of the land, symbolized by the maiden. As is the case with so many of the Maytime and Summer Solstice rituals we have been exploring, the outcome of the inevitable struggle was never seen as a foregone conclusion. In a sense, the battle was new every year, and the ritual reenactment of the struggle for possession of the May Queen was observed with very great seriousness.

Marie Trevelyan in her publication *Folklore and Folk Stories of Wales* gives an account of such mock combat, which was still taking place well into the nineteenth century. An aged Welshman described the battle that is conducted in South Wales in the following way:

When I was a boy, two companies of men and youths were formed. One had for its captain a man dressed in a long coat much trimmed with fur, and on his head a rough fur cap. He carried a stout stick of blackthorn and a kind of shield, on which were studded tufts of wool to represent snow.

A May Day effigy becomes the center of attention in Powderhorn Park, Minneapolis, Minn., U.S.A.

Choosing the May Queen is an important part of May Day celebrations, and the lucky maiden to be picked will be the center of the whole village's joy.

His companions wore caps and waistcoats of fur decorated with balls of white wool. These men were very bold, and in songs and verse proclaimed the virtues of Winter, who was their captain.

The other company had for its leader a captain representing Summer. This man was dressed in a kind of white smock decorated with garlands of flowers and gay ribbons. On his head he wore a broad-brimmed hat trimmed with flowers and ribbons. In his hand he carried a willow-wand wreathed with spring flowers and tied with ribbons. All these men marched in procession, with their captain on horseback leading them, to an appropriate place.

There a mock encounter took place, the Winter company flinging straw and dry wood at their opponents, who used as their weapons birch branches, willow wands, and young ferns. A good deal of horseplay went on, but finally Summer gained the mastery over Winter. Then the victorious captain representing Summer selected a May King and the people nominated a May Queen; they were then crowned and conducted into the village. The remainder of the day was given up to feasting, dancing, games of all kinds, and, later still, drinking. Revelry continued through the night until the next morning.

The choosing and crowning of the May Queen is still an important event, especially in the more rural areas of Northern Europe. Throughout Britain today one can still see white-clad girls carried through the streets on beribboned horses, attended by courtiers dressed in green and white. On arrival at the village green, usually in the shadow of the Maypole, a May Queen chosen from among these girls is enthroned in a special bower, created for her by the young people of the village. She reigns for a year, presiding over community gatherings, much like a queen watching over medieval jousting tournaments.

Through the honoring of such figures, through annual fairs, Maypole dances, and other seasonal observances, the May Day revels continue into our own time the energy of many far older celebrations of the beginning of summer. The May Day games, rituals, and celebrations announce that the sun has passed a major mark on its journey toward its highest point and are a foretaste of the coming great celebrations of Midsummer.

Making a May Day Garland

Traditionally on May Day it was the custom to make floral garlands that were hung either inside the house or outside over the door. These garlands could take almost any form, from a simple circular wreath like those that hang on doors at Christmas, to a cross shape, to a hollow ball that contains tiny dolls representing the May King and Queen.

Creating a May Day garland is quite simple and is a perfect way of celebrating Maytime. First, collect a few springy, pliable branches from a tree such as hazel, elder, sycamore, or ash. Weave these together into whatever shape you feel is most appropriate. You can also weave into the garland a selection of fresh flowers, ribbons, or fruits. Now decide what (if anything) you want to place inside the hollow frame you have created. Attach the chosen objects to the branches using thread. In some areas where this tradition is still active, the figures placed within are the Virgin and Child, connecting later Christian symbolism to the older traditions. You can also use dolls or other figures that represent the masculine and feminine energies of the season.

Next, decorate the garland with blossoms. Any fresh seasonal blooms are appropriate, such as primroses, bluebells, cowslips, or marigolds, though it is advisable never to use actual mayblossoms (hawthorn), as this flower is sacred to the fairy people. The hawthorn is often traditionally associated with death because of its growth in many churchyards.

Hang your finished garland from the ceiling somewhere in or near the center of the house, drape it outside over the door, or suspend it from a Maypole like a crown, as described below.

If you feel it is appropriate, invoke the blessing of the May Queen on your garland, using your own words or the following formula, as you wish:

I/we ask the blessing of the Queen of May,
That good fortune and a happy life
Attend upon this house
And all who dwell within,
Throughout the coming year—
And for as long as may be in the years to come.

Erecting and Decorating a Maypole

As probably the oldest aspect of the celebration of May Day, there can be no more wonderful project than erecting your own Maypole and dancing around it. At one time virtually every town and village throughout Europe would have had a Maypole in place in time for the May Day games. You can still find such customs in European villages that maintain a link with the past. Many people today have begun to raise Maypoles on their own land. This can be done quite easily.

❧ *First, select a tree. In much the same way that one can still go out into the country to find and cut down a Christmas tree, it is possible to seek out a friendly farmer or landowner and obtain permission to cut down a sapling for the Maypole. However, if this proves difficult, a straight pole of any hard wood, such as may be obtained from a lumberyard, will do just as well. Once the tree has been cut and trimmed, it should be brought home with as much ceremony as possible (get a few friends to join in and bear the tree back home with songs and merriment). Then, dig a hole about a fifth as deep as the length of the pole. Sink the pole in the earth and pack earth down firmly around it. A couple of heavy stones placed against the pole may be used to anchor it more firmly.*

❧ *Once in place, the pole is ready for decoration. If you wish, you can hang your May Day garland from the top of the pole. You will also need wide ribbons long enough to stretch from the tip of the pole to the ground when hanging straight. These should be fastened to the top of the pole with nails or staples so they are held firmly in place. Traditionally, the ribbons are red, white, and green (red for blood, white for air, green for earth). The ribbons should be long enough to hold from about six feet away from the pole so you can move in a circular motion around it. There should be one ribbon for each dancer—not too many, or you risk colliding with each other!*

❧ *On May Day, invite your friends and neighbors to join in a celebration. Each dancer takes a ribbon in their hand and dances around the Maypole in a sunwise direction. Any lively music will do, though folk dances are preferable. Properly choreographed, dancers circle in groups or separately with a slight space in time between each so that the ribbons are woven around the pole. Once the ribbons are tightly woven, the dance is reversed and the ribbons unwound again. Thus the symbolic rising and setting of the Midsummer sun is enacted by everyone.*

❧ *Invite the dancers to hold in mind the intentions they would like to see bear fruit over the rest of the year, or to renew their New Year resolutions, invoking the energy of the sun at its most powerful to help them bring their hopes and plans to fruition. Follow your Maypole dance with refreshments, live music, and games.*

Chapter Four

MIDSUMMER NIGHTS AND DAYS

When Midsummer comes,
with bavens and brooms
they do bonfires make,
and swiftly, then,
the nimble young men
run leaping over the same.
The women and maidens
together do couple their hands.
With bagpipes' sound,
they dance a round;
no malice among them stands.

ELIZABETHAN BALLAD, ANON.

Sacred Fires, Sacred Hills, Sacred Springs

Folk celebrations of the Summer Solstice on June 21, and of Midsummer Day on June 22, were similar to the festive observances of May Day, but their energy and intent was deeper and more serious. Many of the outward rituals were the same—the lighting of fires, people and animals jumping or being driven through the flames, communal dancing and singing—and all had the similar intention of driving away evil forces and encouraging the well-being of the sun in its course though the heavens. Yet, especially in northern regions, the Midsummer fires were larger, and the signs and portents in the skies were watched more carefully. From this day forward, people knew, the days would shorten, and the sun's power would wane. The encroaching darkness of the northern skies seemed threatening, and the sparks flying upward from bonfires across the land spelled out meanings known only to the wise.

Perhaps due to the astronomical significance of the solstice, the connection between human beings and the natural forces of the Earth was deemed especially important at this time, and visiting a sacred site to celebrate the solstice was considered particularly meaningful. Throughout the British Isles, people took to the hills to light their Midsummer fires and observe the solstice in other ways. On the eve of Midsummer revelers would climb a hill in the Quantocks, make a pile of stones, and put a bunch of flowers on it for luck.

> On Midsummer Day, standing stones became the focus of sacred observances.

Equally important places of observance were sacred springs and standing stones, which became the focus for Midsummer gatherings across the country. The earliest written record of a Midsummer festival beside a spring comes from a thirteenth-century document. It mentions a charter granted to Barnwell Priory near Cambridge, England, in 1229 for a piece of land on which an annual country fair took place. The fair was held on that particular site, according to the document, because children ("bairns") would gather there for games and sports on St. John the Baptist's Eve (Midsummer), close to an ancient holy well, which became known as Bairn-well.

...from the midst of that site there bubbled forth springs of clear fresh water, called at that time in English, Barnewell, the children's springs, because once a year, on St. John the Baptist's Eve, boys and youths met there, and amused themselves in the English fashion with wrestling matches and other games, and applauded each other in singing songs and playing on musical instruments. Hence by reason of the crowds of boys and girls who met and played there, a habit grew up that on the same day a crowd of buyers and sellers should meet in the same place to do business.

Beautifully made objects like this Celtic spearhead were thrown into sacred wells to please the gods.

> *Get up, get up for shame, the Blooming Morne*
> *Upon her wings presents the god unshorne.*
> *See how Aurora throwes her faire*
> *Fresh, quilted colors through the aire:*
> *Get up, sweet, Slug-a-bed, and see*
> *The Dew-bespangling Herbe and Tree.*
>
> ROBERT HERRICK

limestone that stood in a field next to the parish church, smearing it with sheep salve, tar, or butter; covering it with rags of various colors; and finally decorating its top with seasonal flowers.

Holy wells were especially potent sites for ritual gatherings. A tradition of throwing objects into a well or spring believed to be sacred to a local deity dates back to Celtic times, when beautifully crafted objects, such as swords and horse harnesses, were offered to the gods of rivers and streams. In Yorkshire, the people of Pickering gathered at Midsummer at Newton Dale Well to perform ceremonies that they believed would ensure them the blessings of the well throughout the year. In Northumberland, Bede's Well, near Jarrow, was thought to have strong curative properties, and sick children were dipped into it in the hope of a miraculous cure.

Similarly, on Midsummer Day, standing stones became the focus of sacred observances. In Leicester, families went to a hollow in the nearby hills where children played around St. John's Stone, a seven-foot high pillar believed to possess supernatural powers. Near Sennen in Cornwall, youngsters danced around a Midsummer fire laid on a table-shaped stone called Carrack Sans, and at Urswick, in what was then Lancashire, people decorated a rough piece of unhewn

An ancient yew tree stands guard over the holy well in the Gwenlais valley in South Wales, U.K.

Midsummer celebrations took place on the hill above the mighty Cerne Abbas Giant, Dorset, U.K.

rose on Midsummer morning, an unearthly figure known simply as "The Shining One" walked the ninety-yard avenue of stones leading to the center of the circle. This tradition suggests a distant memory of a time when a sun god, under whatever name, walked the earth at Midsummer. An invocation, collected in nineteenth-century Scotland, but reflecting a more ancient time, speaks to the awe people felt at the divine power and majesty of the Midsummer sun, here honored in female form:

Dancing at the Stones

Several of the most famous prehistoric monuments in Britain had their own Midsummer festivities. William Stukeley, writing in the mid-eighteenth century, suggested that such festivals were continuations of rituals that had originated in pagan times. We have evidence of many such observances. A large fair used to be held at the solstice just south of Boroughbridge in Yorkshire, not far from a line of three enormous monoliths known as the Devil's Arrows. A similar event took place in Dorset at the huge chalk hill carving known as the Cerne Abbas Giant. This mighty figure, which dates from ancient times, was associated with fertility. Celebrations held here acknowledged human sexuality as well as the fertility of the earth.

On the Hebridean island of Lewis, despite opposition from the Church, Midsummer assemblies persisted down to the last century at Scotland's most spectacular megalithic site, the Calanish standing stones. There, according to local legend, when the sun

Hail, O sun of the seasons,
Traverser of the wide skies;
Your steps are strong on the wing of heaven,
O glorious mother of the stars.

In the depths of the ocean you lie,
Without impairment and without fear;
You rise again on the peaceful wave-crest
Like a queenly maiden in bloom.

The Lord and Lady of Summer

Ruling over many countryside Midsummer festivals were the Lord and Lady of Summer. These figures represented the power and fertility of the sun, whose fecund warmth brought life to the earth and ripened the grain. Sometimes these roles were enacted by the same people who played the May King and Queen, but this was not always so. When new actors were chosen, the selection often involved games, sports, and other lively rivalries. However, unlike the struggle between Winter and Summer that lay at the heart of the May Day games, the spirit of these contests was celebration.

The nature of the contests varied from district to district. In Launceston in Cornwall, a large prehistoric mound surrounded by a ditch was the site of annual solstice games. Every Midsummer Eve until the end of the nineteenth century, a large pole was set up at the top of the mound, with a bush fixed at its top. Around this, fuel was heaped and a large bonfire set ablaze.

Against this dramatic backdrop wrestlers contended for various prizes, including the right to rule as Midsummer King. A nineteenth-century observer of this gathering noted that on one previous occasion, an evil spirit appeared in the shape of a black dog, and that since that time no one could wrestle, even in jest, without being injured. As a consequence of this apparition, the practice of wrestling had almost ceased in that area. Interestingly, local tradition held that giants, who had themselves been great wrestlers, were buried in the tumulus.

Contests for women usually took the form of races. Local records for the village of Kidlington in Oxfordshire describe one such competition. It seems that girls of the village, with their thumbs tied behind them, would chase a live lamb around a field. The first to

Local tradition tells of the appearance of King Arthur on Midsummer's Eve here at Cadbury Castle in Somerset, U.K.

catch the animal using only her teeth was declared "Lady of the Lamb." The animal was then slaughtered and its pelt attached to a long pole that was carried like a standard before the Lady and her companions to the village green. The next day the lamb was ceremonially cooked—part baked, part boiled, and part roasted—for the Lady's feast, at which she sat in splendor at the upper end of a table, while "courtiers" played music and everyone spent the day in dancing and merriment.

Sometimes the prize for winning a race was a garland woven of sacred blossoms. These so-called "garland races" survived as an annual custom in Britain well into the nineteenth century. At Askrigg, in Yorkshire, contestants ran up a steep hillside called a "garland course." At Grinton, also in Yorkshire, Midsummer Day was devoted to sports in the afternoon and dancing at night. The winner of the main event, a foot race up a steep hillside, was awarded a prize garland that was then hung in the parish church. At Yarnton in Oxfordshire, youths ran for a garland that the victor displayed in the local church until the following summer, as a symbol of his year-long reign as champion.

Lying behind these more contemporary summer monarchs is the archetypal Summer King, the legendary Arthur. On Midsummer's Eve at Cadbury Castle in Somerset, King Arthur and his knights are said to ride out of the hill beneath the castle. According to local legend, on one occasion the king's horse cast a silver shoe, which was later found and preserved. The story goes on to say that the King required the services of a blacksmith, and that he found one at the nearby prehistoric mound of Wayland's Smithy. The great smith-god Wayland himself, it was said, carried out the task. To this day, local belief holds that if you leave your horse and a silver coin at the Smithy, the next morning you will find it finely shod.

Then joining in a dance
They jig it o'er the green;
Though tired with their labor,
No one less was seen.
But sporting like some fairies,
Their dance they did pursue,
In leading up, and casting off,
Till morning was in view.
And when that bright daylight,
The morning it was come
They lay down and rested
Till the rising of the sun.

ANON.

The Lord of Misrule

Sometimes the Summer King played his part in the style of a Lord of Misrule, similar to the figure who reigned over Midwinter celebrations. The Lord of Misrule was a people's king, elected by them for the brief period of the solstice and given powers that mocked those of Church and state. As such, he represented freedom and license, and an escape from religious piety and the oppressive power of the nobility.

A contemporary account paints a vivid picture of the role of the Lord (and Lady) of Misrule at a typical Midsummer celebration in the late Middle Ages:

Two persons are chosen previous to the meeting to be Lord and Lady of [Mis]Rule, who dress as suitably as they can to the characters they assume. A large empty barn, or some such building, is provided for the Lord's hall, and fitted up with seats to accommodate the company. Here they assemble to dance and regale in the best manner their circumstances and the place will afford. Each young fellow treats his girl with a ribbon or favor; the Lord and Lady honor the hall with their presence, attended by steward, sword-bearer, and mace-bearer, with their several badges or ensigns of office. They have likewise a page and train-bearer, and a jester dressed in part-colored jacket, whose ribaldry and gesticulation contribute not a little to the entertainment of the company.

Judging from the degree of suspicion with which they were regarded by the Church, these celebrations must have been wild indeed. In 1576, an investigation was launched by one Archbishop Grindall, as to:

...whether the ministers and churchwardens have suffered any lords of misrule or summer lords and ladies, or any disguised personage or others...to come unreverently into the church or churchyard and there to dance or to play any unseemly parts, with scoffs, jests, wanton gestures, or ribald talking.

Similar attacks took place throughout the Middle Ages and into the sixteenth and seventeenth centuries, but they did nothing to stop the yearly gatherings to celebrate Midsummer.

In our day, the characters of the old Midsummer pageants are playing out their roles in new ways. Since 1999, the villagers of Aston Cantlow in Warwickshire have put on a Midsummer festival that features the wedding procession of the Green Man and Lady. The pageant begins at the gate of the church of St. John the Baptist with a celebration of the marriage of these archetypal figures, in whom we can see reflected both the May King and Queen and the Lord and Lady of Summer. The procession then circles the church, led by the figure of Robin Goodfellow and followed by the

The Lord and Lady of Summer proceed to the Wedding of the Green Man and Lady at Aston Cantlow, Warwickshire, U.K.

Green Man Morris Team. Aston Cantlow itself has some interesting associations. William Shakespeare's parents are said to have married there, and the church has a fourteenth-century carving of a Green Man, which some believe may have inspired Shakespeare's own celebration of Midsummer madness.

Midsummer Night's Dreaming

Shakespeare's knowledge of fairy lore was extensive and, especially in his early plays, it yielded many memorable themes and characters. Perhaps the best-known evocation of the magic of Midsummer is the comedy *A Midsummer Night's Dream*. In the play, Theseus, the Duke of Athens, is about to wed Hippolyta, the Queen of the Amazons. The royal couple is paralleled by two sets of less happily paired lovers. A young Athenian girl, Hermia, has been promised by her father to Demetrius, but she loves another young man, Lysander. When Hermia and Lysander run away to the woods around Athens to avoid her marriage, Demetrius follows them. He is, in turn, followed by Helena, another young Athenian woman who loves Demetrius though he scorns her.

In the woods, the four young people become entwined in an argument between Oberon, the King of the Fairies, and Titania, the Fairy Queen—the archetypal Lord and Lady of Summer. The fairies have come to the wood to hold their Midsummer revels and to bless the marriage of Theseus and Hippolyta. On Midsummer Night, the fairy kingdom collides with the mortal world with hilarious results. A magic flower, with the power to make the person on whose sleeping eyelids it is applied fall madly in love with whatever creature is seen upon awakening, is dropped on the wrong eyes by the mischievous sprite Puck, also

left
Puck and the fairies in a
1999 production of Shakespeare's
A Midsummer Night's Dream.

below
Robin Goodfellow still haunts the
woods in Midsummer celebrations
at Aston Cantlow, Warwickshire, U.K.

known as Robin Goodfellow. Confusion reigns, and for a time, both Lysander and Demetrius forsake their devotion to Hermia and dote on Helena. At the instigation of the King of the Fairies, even the Fairy Queen Titania is bewitched by the love potion. It makes her fall in love with Bottom, a buffoonish

weaver, who has repaired to the woods with a group of fellow Athenian workingmen to rehearse a play to be performed at the Duke's wedding. To complete the Fairy Queen's humiliation, Bottom is transformed by Puck so that he sports the head of an ass.

In the end, everything is sorted out properly, of course. The wedding of Theseus and Hippolyta is celebrated, along with the marriages of Hermia and Lysander, and of Helena and Demetrius. The King and Queen of the Fairies, newly reconciled, bless the marriages and the potential offspring that will hopefully result from the wedding night fun:

Now, until the break of day,
Through the house each fairy stray
To the best bride-bed will we,
Which by us shall blessèd be;
And the issue there create
Ever shall be fortunate.
So shall all the couples three
Ever true in loving be.

(act 5, scene 1)

Shakespeare's play draws on the tradition that at Midsummer, the veils between the worlds are thin, and the Otherworld intersects with this one. Midsummer Night was a time for dreams in which portents of the future might be seen; for trickster spirits like Puck (his name probably derives from the Middle English *pook* or *pouke*, meaning "elf" or "sprite") to lead night-wanderers astray; for magical transformations; and for enchantments, such as the little purple flower that can make people fall instantly in love. Though Shakespeare set his play in ancient Greece rather than the British countryside, the mood of comic revelry and fairy magic that pervades it is thoroughly in keeping with the celebrations of Midsummer we have been examining throughout this chapter.

Magical Ferns

Magical plants, like the purple flower of Shakespeare's play, have their own traditions in solstice lore. It was believed that a certain mysterious fern, popularly known as the "treasure fist," "death plant," or "death flower," bloomed and produced seed only during the night of the Summer Solstice—and, some added, only once every hundred years. According to a seventeenth-century herbal, this fern carries its tiny seeds on the backs of its leaves. Anyone who succeeded in collecting the seeds could use them to become invisible. This curious piece of herbal lore is referred to in Shakespeare's *Henry IV, Part 1*, when Gadshill says: "We have the recipe of fern-seed, we walk invisible."

Many folk traditions held that ferns had magical powers —those that flowered on Midsummer night were supposed to make people invisible.

Those who had the courage went into the woods at midnight on the solstice to seek these seeds, though it was said that evil spirits kept at bay anyone who searched for them. In northern regions, when night became as light as day at Midsummer, the bloom of the fern was said to glow like an ember, its spectral appearance announced by thunder. The Finns believed that those most likely to find the seeds were orphan children, presumably because they might be fairy changelings. Finnish folk traditions held that the fern seeds were guarded by trolls and other strange beings, who would snatch them away from anyone foolish enough to quest for the wealth and magic powers the seeds might bring, or make the seeker go insane.

In Ireland a story is told of a man who went to gather fern seeds and reported that spirits whispered in his ears and sometimes struck his hat and other parts of his body. When the man thought he had gathered enough, he secured the magical seeds in a box, only to find the box empty when he arrived home. In Britain, it was believed that the seeds could be gathered only on pewter plates—some said eleven pewter plates, since the seeds had the property of passing through all the others.

Seeing the Future

Perhaps because the Summer Solstice was such an important turning point in the year, the period around Midsummer ushered in a positive frenzy of divination. An oracle of hempseed was consulted by young men and women desiring to see whom they would marry. They circumambulated the church in a sunwise direction, throwing handfuls of hempseed over one shoulder, all the while chanting:

Hempseed I sow, hempseed I hoe,
Let him/her that is my true love come after me
*   and mow.*

Everywhere girls plucked flowers to see if their lovers were faithful. If the flowers wilted or the petals came apart, the flower brought bad news; if they bent inward toward each other, the prospects for faithful love were good. Another divinatory practice was to melt pieces of lead or solder and drop them into a pan of cold water. The molten metal spread into curious shapes that could be studied and read for their hidden meanings.

Roses, too, were believed to be magical when gathered on Midsummer Eve. Such blooms were said to keep fresh until Christmas. Girls who wanted to discover the identity of future lovers scattered these rose petals in front of them, chanting:

Rose leaves, rose leaves,
Rose leaves I strew.
He that will love me
Come after me now.

Midsummer night seems always to have been a night for love magic, just as in Shakespeare's play. Women desiring children rolled in the dewy grass on Midsummer morning to aid fertility. The Midsummer dew was also believed to banish freckles and sunburn and heal all skin diseases. Young girls believed that if they gathered nine different kinds of herbs and put them under their pillow, they would see their future groom in their dreams. In France and Germany, young girls believed that if they looked into a holy well at midnight on Midsummer night, they would see reflected the face of the man they were to marry.

left
Roses that bloomed at Midsummer were believed to be especially magical.

below
During Midsummer girls would collect flowers and herbs, in the hope of seeing their future love.

The Feast of St. John the Baptist

As we saw in chapter three, many seasonal festivals were adapted to mark important dates in the Christian calendar. Thus, close upon Midsummer Day, the feast day of St. John the Baptist on June 24 became associated with the games and celebrations of Midsummer. Something of a two-way traffic took place between the two events, with aspects of the earlier pagan rites mingling almost seamlessly with those that constellated about the figure of the saint.

This joining was due in part to the actions of a seventh-century pope, Gregory the Great. He instructed those emissaries of the Church whose task it was to carry the Christian message to Northern Europe not to destroy the old pagan shrines but to rededicate them to the new God:

In this way, I hope the people [seeing their temples are not destroyed] will leave their idolatry and yet continue to frequent the places as formerly…on such high [feast] days the people might well build themselves shelters of boughs round the churches that were once temples and celebrate the occasion with pious feasting. They must no more sacrifice animals to the Devil, but they may kill them for food.

The consequence of this enlightened instruction was less the desired "pious feasting" than the perpetuation of traditional festivals, which came to be celebrated in churchyards rather than ancestral shrines. This overlapping of the two traditions became a constant source of friction between clergy and parishioners for well over a thousand years.

The fact that Church and state were powerless to prevent such celebrations is evident from the attempts at suppression that persisted throughout most of the medieval period. In the tenth century, rituals that centered around springs, hills, trees, and stones, and those celebrating May Day and Midsummer, were forbidden by King Edgar of England. Again, some fifty years later, the Laws of Canute banned the worship of "water wells or stones, or any kind of wood trees." In 1409, the Bishop of Hereford ordered a proclamation to be read in every church in his diocese against those who worshiped a stone and well in the parish of Turnastone:

It has come to our ears, we grieve to say, from the report of many credible witnesses and the common report of the people, that many of our subjects are in large numbers visiting a certain well and stone at Turnastone in our diocese where with genuflections and offerings they without authority of the church wrongfully worship the said stone and well, whereby committing idolatry; when the water fails they take away with them the mud of the same and treat and keep it as a relic to the grave peril of their souls and a pernicious example to others. Therefore we suspend the use of the said well and stone and under pain of greater excommunication forbid our people to visit the well and stone for the purpose of worship.

Yet when we look at medieval accounts of celebrations of the Summer Solstice and the Feast of St. John, it is hard to see where one begins and the other ends. Thus the author of *The Comical Pilgrim's Pilgrimage into Ireland* (1787) remarks:

On the vigil of St. John the Baptist's Nativity, [people] make Bonfires, and run along the streets and fields with wisps of straw blazing on long poles to purify the air, which they think infectious, by believing all the

> The Laws of Canute banned the worship of "water wells or stones, or any kind of wood trees."

devils, spirits, ghosts, and hobgoblins fly abroad this night to hurt mankind. Furthermore, it is their theology to affirm the souls of all people leave their bodies on the Eve of this Feast, and take their ramble to that very place, where, by land or sea, a final separation shall divorce them for evermore in this world.

Here, again, we see the belief that on Midsummer night, the spirits of the dead, as well as other beings both friendly and malevolent, are abroad.

A medieval church calendar gives us some idea of what was considered appropriate to the feast of St. John the Baptist. Some curious inclusions demonstrate just how thoroughly the old and new ways had merged.

June 23rd: The Vigil of John the Baptist.
Spices are given at Vespers.
Fires are lighted up.
A girl with a little drum proclaims the Garland.
Boys are dressed in girls' clothes.
Carols to the liberal; imprecations against the
    avaricious.
Waters are swum in during the night, and are brought
    [inside] in vessels that hang for purposes of
    divination.
Fern [is] in great estimation with the vulgar on
    account of its seed.
Herbs of different kinds are sought, with many
    ceremonies.

The same mixture of Christian and pagan observances is found in Scotland. There, especially among the people of the Hebridean Isles in the nineteenth century, men still uncovered their heads when they saw the sun rising in the morning. A story recorded at this time by the great collector Alexander Carmichael tells of a pious man, whose observances are a blend of Christian and solar worship:

There was a man in Arasaig, and he was extremely old, and he would make adoration to the sun and to the moon and to the stars. When the sun would rise on the tops of the peaks, he would put off his head covering and he would bow down his head, giving glory to the great God of life for the glory of the sun and for the goodness of its light to the children of men

This thirteenth-century Byzantine icon shows St. John the Baptist, whose birthday falls on June 24 and is celebrated at Midsummer.

and to the animals of the world. When the sun set in the western ocean, the old man would again take off his head covering, and he would bow his head to the ground and say:

I am in hope, in its proper time,
That the great and gracious God
Will not put out for me the light of grace
Even as thou dost leave me this night.

Wheels of Fire

Another solstice custom that mingled people's reverence for the sun with a later Christian message is the rolling of fiery wheels down from the heights. At the Summer Solstice, the fiery wheels represented the sun—then occupying the highest place in the heavens—beginning its descent. A similar custom at the Winter Solstice signified the return of the sun at the darkest time of the year. The seventeenth-century poet of the seasons, Naogeorgus, explains that special wheels were covered with straw, set on fire, and rolled down a mountain, so that it appeared from a distance as if the sun had fallen from the sky and was rolling along the horizon. He notes that people believed that their ill luck was taken away by this action.

This practice dated back at least as early as the fourth century, where we find it mentioned in the Acts of St. Vincent as a ritual followed by the pagan community of Aquitaine in southern France. There the fiery wheel was rolled down into a river, and afterward, the charred and broken pieces were reassembled and displayed for all to see in the temple of the local god. Similar rituals were described around 530 C.E. by a British monk at Winchcombe in Gloucestershire.

However, the association of St. John the Baptist with Midsummer fires is underscored in a number of

This dramatic image shows barrels of flaming tar being rolled downhill at Ottery St. Mary, Devon, U.K.

texts, perhaps nowhere more so than in a curious medieval work entitled *Homily De Festo Sancti Johannis Baptistae*. Here, we read:

In worship of Saint John the people...made three kinds of fire: one is [of] clean bones, and no wood, and that is called a Bone Fire; another is [of] clean wood, and no bones, and that is called a Wood Fire; ...the third is made of wood and bones, and it is called Saint John's Fire.

The text adds some intriguing details as to the nature of each fire. The Bone Fire was designed to drive away dragons, who hate the stench of burning bones above all else. The Wood Fire burned especially bright in token of the spiritual fires that burned within the great Apostle, here described as "a lantern light to the people." The third, Saint John's Fire, of bones and wood together, "betokens the Saint's martyrdom, for his bones were burned." The writer accounts for this rather curious statement by telling us that after John's disciples had buried his body, it lay undisturbed until Julian, the apostate Emperor, caused them to be taken up and burned, "and to cast the ashes in the wind, hoping that he should never rise again to life." Thus the fires long associated with the solstice and the fires of Christian martyrdom were mixed and mingled.

A Contemporary Solstice Festival

Today one of the foremost celebrations that recognizes both St. John and the solstice is the Golowan Festival, which takes place in the small town of Penzance in Cornwall. The name *Golowan* comes from the Cornish *Gol-Jowan* (The Feast of John). Though the actual origins of this festival are, even to its current organizers, lost in the mists of time, the energy, color, and unquestionable power of the celebrations, which take place over the week in which June 22 falls, are probably as near as we will ever get in our time to catching a glimpse of a more ancient solstice festival. Among the events that take place are the election of a Mock Mayor, a clear harking back to the Lord of Misrule figure; the rolling of lighted wheels like those described above; and the performance of a wild "Serpent Dance," which probably dates back to the ancient celebration of the dragon or serpent energy long perceived as a source of power within the land.

Celebrations of this kind, which still take place throughout Europe, are a genuine continuation of far older festivals of the Summer Solstice. They help preserve the age-old wish of humankind to honor the sun and to bless its continued presence in the lives of people everywhere.

Mazy Day takes place during the Golowan Festival in Penzance, Cornwall, U.K.

A Midsummer Feast

There is no better way to celebrate Midsummer than with a party. And, since the event is to be a ritual occasion as well as a celebration, you'll want to include both sacred and festive elements, including a bonfire, appropriate games, stories, and entertainment, and traditional food.

❧ PREPARING THE SITE. *Selecting a location for your gathering is the first step. You'll need room to build a fire and space for dancing, storytelling, feasting, and other activities. If you have private land in the countryside, it is ideal. A public park or forest preserve site that allows open fires and private parties would also be suitable. You might also consider inviting your neighbors to collaborate in a communal event or seeking permission to add some solstice-honoring activities to an already established summer fair or festival in your village or town, or one sponsored by a local church or school.*

❧ LIGHTING THE FIRE. *Choose and prepare the site for your Midsummer fire carefully. You may want to dig a proper fire pit, if a natural dip in the ground does not already exist. It should be deep enough to contain the foundations of the fire and well lined with flat stones around both sides and bottom to form a safe base. Next you should consider what wood you will use. It is wisest, for both ecological and spiritual reasons, to use only wood that has already fallen from trees. If you do need to cut any branches, be certain that you do so wisely, thanking the tree for its gift. Lay the logs with care, heaviest at the bottom, so the fire will not collapse once it is lit.*

Before you light the fire, whether you are alone or with friends, take a few moments to sit quietly and tune into your reasons for creating this event. Think about the nature of the Summer Solstice and all that it means and has meant to humanity since we first made homes for ourselves in caves. When the time is right, and everyone is assembled, light the fire, thinking of all those who are doing the same thing in different places and different time zones around the world. Perhaps repeat an invocation, such as the one that follows:

*I light this fire
in the spirit of all those
who have lit fires on this night,
and I call upon the spirits of the Solstice
to be present and to bless this fire.*

SONGS AND DANCES. This is a night very much meant for dancing and song. The following, from the Elizabethan period, captures the lighthearted quality of the festival:

On a fair morning, as I came by the way,
Met I with a merry maid in the merry month of May,
When a sweet love sings his lovely lay
And every bird upon the bush bechirps it up so gay
With a heave and ho! with a heave and ho!
Thy wife shall be thy master, I trow.
Sing, care away, care away, let the world go!
Hey, lustily all in a row, all in a row,
Sing, care away, care away, let the world go!
THOMAS MORLEY

FIRE LEAPING. If you can do so safely (with enough space on either side of the fire), you might want to follow the age-old practice of jumping over the embers of the fire. Be sure to jump only when the fire has burned low and avoid loose or flammable clothing! Jump over the fire as a ritual act, with intention. For instance, before jumping, ask a question of the gods of Midsummer and watch for an answer on the other side.

STORYTELLING. The magic of Midsummer Night would not be complete without stories. Throughout this book you will find tales from different parts of the world. You might try learning one of these by heart, then telling it to your guests by the light of the fire. Of course there are many hundreds of other tales connected to the Summer Solstice. You will find books listed in the Further Reading section that contain excellent retellings of many such tales. You might even find yourself inspired to write a story of your own. Whatever you do, make the telling as special as you can. If you have a friend who can accompany you on a musical instrument, so much the better.

GIFTS FOR THE FAIRIES. Children have always left out gifts for the fairies, and this simple act can still be an important event in any family gathering. Some people, especially in Scandinavia, make elaborate shapes from bread or pastry and hang them from a tree or bush near the house. Or, you may simply place a few fancy cakes decorated with tiny silver balls on a plate. These small offerings are always gone by morning and ensure the goodwill and blessings of the fairy folk through the year.

FOOD FOR THE FEAST. Overleaf are a couple of recipes for dishes traditionally served at Midsummer. You will find others once you start searching. Ask older people if they have any special recipes for this time of year. You will soon build up your own recipe collection.

MIDSUMMER SYLLABUB

Syllabub is a refreshing light dessert combining the cream and cider of village produce.

¼ pt or 150 ml of dry cider or apple juice
Rind and juice of 1 lemon
1 oz or 25 g superfine (caster) sugar
½ tsp of grated nutmeg
¼ pt or 150 ml of light cream
¼ pt or 150 ml of heavy or whipping cream
(double cream)
Sprig of fresh mint or candied angelica (optional)

Combine the cider or apple juice with the lemon rind in a large bowl. Stir in the sugar and nutmeg. Pour in the light cream and the double (heavy) cream. Whisk in the bowl (or food processor) until the mixture starts to thicken and then add the lemon juice. Whisk briefly again. Spoon it into individual dishes—glasses are especially nice—and chill well in the refrigerator for at least two hours. Decorate the top, just before serving, with a sprig of fresh mint or some candied angelica leaves.

You can also make this dessert with summer fruits, such as strawberries or gooseberries. Simply place the berries or small pieces of fruit at the bottom of the serving glass before spooning on the syllabub cream.

QUEEN MAB'S SUMMER PUDDING

Summer Pudding is an old English specialty that is still popular today. The lightness of the pudding, combined with the vibrancy of the freshly gathered fruits, make it a wonderful Midsummer dish.

6–8 slices of slightly stale white bread,
*   with the crusts cut off*
1½ lbs or 750 g of soft fruits, such as
*   blackcurrants, strawberries, blueberries,*
*   raspberries, etc.*
2 tbsp water
5 oz or 150 g of sugar
whipped cream

Line a medium-sized bowl with some slices of bread, making sure to cover the bottom and sides completely. Wash and prepare the fruit and put it into a saucepan with the water and sugar. Boil slowly until the sugar melts and the juices begin to run, but do not allow the fruit to disintegrate. Spoon the fruit into the prepared dish and cover it with a lid of the remaining bread. Put a saucer or small plate that fits inside the dish on top and weigh it down with a heavy can or jar. Chill for a minimum of eight hours. Remove the can or jar and plate. Take a knife and carefully run it around the inside edge of the bowl and turn out the pudding onto a dish. Serve with whipped cream.

Chapter Five

GODS OF THE HARVEST

John Barleycorn's a hero bold as any in the land
For ages good his fame has stood and
shall for ages stand
The whole wide world respect in him,
no matter friend or foe
And where they be that makes so free
he's sure to lay them low.

TRADITIONAL

Gods of the Field

As the year moved onward and the high days of summer grew shorter, a somber note entered into the games and celebrations that encouraged the turning seasons. In the days between Midsummer and Harvest—roughly July to September—the focus of agricultural activity shifted to collecting the last fruits of summer and planting next year's crop, while the seasonal mysteries centered around the notion of sacrifice, the needful offerings to the gods of the harvest, and a celebration of the harvest itself.

Powerful and mysterious spirits ruled over the fields at this time. Perhaps the most poignant is the God of the Harvest, an ancient being who literally embodies the sustenance promised by the harvested crops.

In Egypt he is celebrated in the person of Osiris, the dying and rising god of the Nile Delta. Osiris was killed and dismembered by Seth, the god of chaos and disorder, but his faithful wife Isis searched for his scattered bones and restored him to potency. His resurrection mirrors the annual miracle of returning life in the desert. To this day in Egypt, in the dark time of the year, miniature sarcophagi are planted with seeds that sprout green shoots through spring and summer, a visible reminder of the miracle of life from death that lies at the heart of the agricultural year.

Ancient gods of the harvest were also revered in Europe and the Americas. The following old English folk song, probably dating from the days before such songs were written down, tells the story of a British

The Egyptian god Osiris (center) flanked by his wife Isis and his son Horus. (New Kingdom, ninth century B.C.E.)

harvest god, John Barleycorn. It is his sacrifice and suffering that provide the staples of daily fare, for from his "bones" come bread and beer.

There were three men came out of the West
Their fortunes for to try,
And these three men made a solemn vow,
John Barleycorn should die.

They plowed him in the earth so deep,
With clods upon his head,
Then these three men they did conclude
John Barleycorn was dead.

There he lay sleeping in the ground
Till rain from the sky did fall,
Then Barleycorn sprang a green blade
And proved liars of them all.

There he remained till Midsummer
And looked both pale and wan.
Then Barleycorn grew a long, long beard
Much like unto a man.

They hired men with scythes so sharp
To cut him off at the knee.
See how they served poor Barleycorn
They served him bitterly.

They hired men with forks and rakes
To pierce him through to the heart,
But the carter served him worse than that
For he bound him to a cart.

And then they brought him to a barn
A prisoner to endure,
And soon they fetched him out again
And laid him on the floor.

They hired men with crabtree sticks
To beat him flesh from bones,
But the miller served him worse than that
For he ground him 'tween two stones.

They flung him into a cistern deep
And drowned him in water clean,
But the brewer served him worse than that
For he brewed him into beer.

Oh Barleycorn is the very best grain
That ever was sown on land.
It will serve you more than any grain
From the turning of your hand.

Mysterious and never represented as an image, cut down, threshed, flailed and beaten, ground, and made into bread and ale, John Barleycorn is warmed by the rays of the sun and rises triumphant again in the spring, as have corn gods the world over.

The Dressing of the Goddess

Farther south in ancient Greece, a high point of the sacred year was a huge public festival called the Panathenaea, which took place during the heart of summer, from the 21st to the 28th of the month of Hecatombaion, bridging our July and August. At this spectacular event, the traditional birthday of Athena, Homeric hymns were recited to honor the Olympian gods, and contests and games were staged. On the first three days were musical competitions; then came athletic and gymnastic exercises, including boxing and wrestling matches, horse and chariot races. The festival

concluded with a torchlight procession and sacrifices in Athena's main temple, the Parthenon.

The whole pageant is vividly depicted on the famous Parthenon frieze known as the Elgin Marbles. The west frieze depicts the preparations for the procession, which starts from the southwest corner of the Parthenon in two groups, heading in either direction to meet in the east. In the first grouping, horsemen and their attendants are outfitting themselves and their horses, fastening boots and harnesses, and mounting their steeds. Moving northward, the group gets denser as other horsemen appear. On the next slab chariots and armed men join them. In front of the troops are marshals, and though at this point the frieze is badly damaged, it seems that they are led by a group of elders bearing olive branches, musicians playing lyres and flutes, boys carrying water pots for libation and bearing trays of offerings. Before them go the animals for sacrifice with their attendants, led by a heifer. On the east frieze, the streams of the procession converge. Girls carrying jugs, incense, burners, and libation bowls lead the way. Two girls in the center hold stools or cushions on their heads, which are presented to the priestess of Athena, perhaps as seats for the gods.

The priestess of Athena prepares one of the two stools, apparently for the attendant gods, who are seated in two groups. These include Artemis, Apollo, Poseidon with his trident, and Eros holding a parasol over his mother Aphrodite. Athena stands near Hephaestus, without her helmet but holding her breastplate bearing the Gorgon's head. Opposite her is her father Zeus with his wife Hera, while to her left is a young girl with wings, probably Nike. The heavily draped

This detail from the fifth-century Parthenon frieze shows the handing over of the sacred peplos, in which the goddess Athena will be dressed.

The boughs do shake and bells do ring,
So merrily comes our harvest in,
Our harvest in, our harvest in,
So merrily comes our harvest in.

We've plowed we've sowed,
We've reaped, we've mowed,
We've got our harvest in.

ANON.

goddess in front of Ares is Demeter, and opposite her is Dionysus leaning on the shoulder of Hermes.

At the head of each section of the procession are maidens, who may represent those girls of good birth who have been selected to weave a new robe, or *peplos*, which will be draped over the statue of Athena as the centerpiece of the ritual. The peplos is conveyed to the temple on the mast of a ship set on wheels. This vessel, which reminds us of the sun boats in Midsummer celebrations farther north, is not shown on the frieze, but the handing up of the peplos to the priest by a small boy is depicted in the center, directly above the eastern door of the Parthenon. Significantly, the goddess who will receive this new garment is not the huge statue, already dressed in gold and armored with shield and helmet. Rather the goddess to be dressed is a more humble image made of olive wood, ancient beyond reckoning. This Athena is the people's goddess, her annual renewal reminiscent of the agricultural cycles honored in other harvest rites.

The Eleusinian Festivals

By far the most important festivals in Greece were those held annually in honor of Demeter and Kore, the Lesser and Greater Eleusinian Mysteries. In the month of Anthesterion (equivalent to our January/February), the first of these two celebrations was held in a suburb of Athens. In the absence of any traces of a sanctuary or temple, and from the general character of the rites at Eleusis, it seems likely that the Lesser Mysteries were held in the open air to bless the newly sown seed corn. These probably bore some resemblance to the May Day celebrations of Northern Europe and were a time of abandonment and wildness in celebration of the rebirth of the year.

The Greater Eleusinian Mysteries, however, were more serious. They centered around a sacred drama portraying the rape and abduction of the spring maiden Kore (Persephone) by Hades (Pluto), the god of the Underworld, and the wanderings of her sorrowing mother Demeter, goddess of grain and the earth's fertility, in search of her. In her grief over losing her daughter, Demeter forgets to allow the rain to fall, and drought and famine grip the earth.

Disguised as an old woman who has escaped from pirates, Demeter wanders to Eleusis. There, while sitting on a seat covered with a ram's skin by a wayside well, she encounters the daughters of the ruler, Keleos, and is taken by them to their home. Acting as nurse to their infant brother Demophoon, Demeter endeavors secretly to make him immortal by anointing him by day with ambrosia, the food of the gods, and by holding him each night in the fire to consume his mortal nature. Disturbed during this act by the child's mother, who screams in terror at the sight of her son in the flames, Demeter reveals her true identity. Before leaving the royal household, she commands the people of Eleusis to build her a sanctuary on the hill above "the fountain of maidenhood" where she first met the daughters of Keleos. At this site, she will teach her votaries rites that bestow upon them blissful immortality and ensure the fruitfulness of the harvest.

Demeter allows the fructifying rain to fall on the parched ground and the grain to grow.

The drought and famine caused by Demeter's grief at the abduction of her daughter continue until Zeus intervenes and secures Kore's return. Before letting her go, Hades contrives to make the girl eat some pomegranate seeds, which bind her to him for a third of the year. As long as Kore is above ground, Demeter allows the fructifying rain to fall on the parched ground and the grain to grow, but on the return of Kore to the nether regions, drought once more prevails, until her ascent again in October when the crops begin to germinate.

In the fall, while the grain was stored in silos beneath the ground, rites were performed to encourage the renewal of the crops and the return of Kore and her reunion with Demeter. From the 13th to the 22nd of Boedromion, (September/October) the Greater Eleusinian festival took place, beginning with a procession to fetch various sacred artifacts from the sanctuary of Demeter at Eleusis and bring them to Athens. Having undergone preliminary purification, the participants in the Mysteries were scrutinized by priests to ensure that they had fulfilled their ritual preparations, that they could read, write, and speak Greek fluently, and that they had not been deprived of civil rights for murder or similar crimes, these being the conditions required for initiation.

This accomplished, the celebrants were led to the sea at Phaleron to bathe, after which sacred pigs were sacrificed to the goddess. After several days of feasting and ritual, on the 19th, late in the evening, the celebrants were led in procession along the Sacred Way from Athens to Eleusis. On arriving, they again bathed in the sea, then roamed about the shore with lighted torches, enacting Demeter's search for her abducted daughter. In the evening they assembled in darkness and silence, and there, sitting on stools covered with sheepskins, they beheld sacred sights that might never be revealed. The festival ended with everyone present looking up to the sky and calling out "rain," then looking down at the earth and crying "be fruitful."

A number of myths and traditions were incorporated into this complex festival, but behind them lies the veneration of Demeter as the Corn Mother, the goddess of vegetation and fertility, who at Eleusis also becomes the giver of immortality to her initiates. The enactment of the Kore myth almost certainly included the reaping of a single ear of corn in profound silence and a blaze of light, followed in all probability by the enactment of a sacred marriage between one of the hierophants and the chief priestess. This symbolic act reaffirmed the idea of rebirth both in nature and humankind and assured that the wheel of the life cycle would continue to turn. To this day the ruins of Eleusis are haunted by the memory of the ancient rites that once took place there.

The Corn Mother and goddess of fertility and vegetation, Demeter, mourns her lost child Persephone. (Painting by Evelyn de Morgan, 1906)

Harvest Community

Whether the sacred observances involved the great gods and goddesses, or were, more simply, a celebration of earthly fertility, harvest time impacted on the lives of everyone. In places where a rigorous social hierarchy existed, it would vanish during the period of the harvest, and everyone would enter into the spirit of the work and subsequent celebration on an equal basis. Thomas Tusser advised landholders in the fifteenth century to observe this important tradition:

In harvest time, harvest-folk, servants and all
Should make all together good cheer in thy hall.
Once ended thy harvest, let none be beguiled
Please such as did help thee, man, woman, and child.

Many harvest traditions originated in the fact that the process of cutting and threshing the grain required the cooperation of the entire community. First, the corn was reaped with handheld sickles or, more recently, with scythes. Then the stalks were tied into sheaves, a task generally given to older men and women, who used cornstalk bands for tying, woven by the children. After this, the sheaves were heaped

Members of an itinerant threshing gang—a familiar sight in late ninteenth-century Britain.

up into stocks to finish ripening. Then they were carted away to be stored in ricks or silos to protect them from inclement weather. But even then, the harvest work was not over, since later the grain had to be threshed or beaten with flails and then winnowed or separated with sieves.

Every step in this process had its own customs, which varied little between one area and another. In Scotland as recently as the 1890s, a visibly pagan tradition continued, as described by the great Gaelic folklorist Alexander Carmichael:

The day the people began to reap the corn was a day of commotion and ceremonial in the townland. The whole family repaired to the field dressed in their best attire to hail the God of the Harvest. Laying his bonnet on the ground, the father of the family took up his sickle, and facing the sun, he cut a handful of corn. Putting the handful of corn three times sunwise round his head, the man raised the Iolach Buana, the reaping salutation. The whole family took up the strain and praised the God of the Harvest, who gave them corn and bread, food and flocks, wool and clothing, health and strength, and peace and plenty.

The Last Sheaf

The cutting of the corn was honored in many places by the creation of corn dolls, figures woven from strands of corn decorated with ribbons and tinsel, representing the Corn Mother and the spirit of harvest. Often these dolls were made from the last sheaf to be cut from the

above
A farmer in Ohio, U.S.A., cradles the last sheaf of corn to be harvested.

left
St. Bridget was acknowledged as the protector of the harvest in Scotland and Ireland.
(Painting by John Duncan)

field. Alternately, it would be tucked under the arm of the corn doll and carried to the Harvest Home supper.

In some places, particularly in the south of England, strands of ivy were threaded through the corn that made up the doll, making her the Ivy Girl. Ivy was a symbol of continued life, the living power that miraculously returned to the fields between one harvest and the next. In many areas the corn doll was kept in the farmhouse until a new one was made at the next harvest, at which time the old doll was brought out and ceremonially burned. In some areas, the Corn Maiden was represented by an actual girl, usually the prettiest in the area, though if the harvest were late, the role might be played by an old woman, representing the Cailleach, or Old One, a primal Mother Goddess dating back centuries.

In Scotland and Ireland, at the festival of the goddess Bride or Bridget (February 1), dolls known as Breide Oggs and made from large stocks of corn were dressed in swaddling bands like babies and laid in baskets called Brides' Beds, which were installed with ceremony in the home. Though the ceremony surrounding these dolls took place away from the period of the harvest, it is not hard to see this ritual as echoing those surrounding the corn dolls. An almost identical practice is recorded as taking place in the Malay Peninsula in the nineteenth century; in this instance, very much a part of the harvest rituals.

The making of corn dolls was only one of several customs surrounding the cutting of the last sheaf. In Ireland particularly there was a great sense of ceremony surrounding this act. There the workers gathered about the final sheaf, in which it was presumed some living creature resided. Often, this was actually the case, as frogs, small animals, partridges, corncrakes, and other birds retreated before the advancing line of reapers until they became trapped in the final sheaf. In many instances the trapped animal was a hare; thus the phrase "putting the hare out of the corn" was understood to mean that the harvest had ended. Often the workers raised a cry to frighten out the creature, and if a farmer

There was a meal of specially baked cakes and ale, accompanied by speech making.

on adjacent land had not yet finished his own harvesting, the hare was said to go there. "We sent you the hare" was a joke aimed at the tardy farmer.

In Britain a ceremony known as "Crying the Neck" accompanied the cutting of the last blades of corn. The reaper, pausing before the last sheaf, called out three times, "I have her," to which everyone present responded with the ritual answer, "What have thee?" The reply was, "A neck, a neck, a neck." At that, the sheaf was cut, put on a specially decorated wagon, and escorted ceremonially to the farmhouse for the celebration of the Harvest Home feast.

Harvest Home

The Harvest Home feast was usually held in the largest barn on the farm. The master and his wife presided over the supper table around which everyone connected with the farm was seated on equal terms. There was a meal of specially baked cakes and ale, accompanied by speech-making and sometimes a visit from elaborately garbed neighbours.

At harvest time, as at the other great festivals of the year, processions of guisers or mummers (people who wore disguises or masks) traveled around the countryside playing tricks on people, offering riddle competitions, putting on plays or pantomimes, and collecting money for charity. In Britain these most often took the form of the hobby-horse procession, which consisted of masked revelers accompanied by a man carrying a horse skull draped in black and sometimes wearing huge hooped skirts to disguise his form. Finland's version was the straw goat procession,

The most experienced and respected mower would be chosen as the Lord of the Harvest and would rule over his gang of mowers like a king.

The spring is like a young maid
That does not know her mind,
The summer is a tyrant
Of most ungracious kind.
The autumn is an old friend
That pleases all he can,
And brings the bearded barley
To glad the heart of man.

ANON

which included a figure covered in a goatskin and adorned with horns, a false beard, and a tail made from a broom. Both images are very ancient and were designed to evoke fear as well as humor.

A similar merrymaking tradition included young men and girls exchanging clothes, breaking into the barn, snatching food, and generally causing disorder. The young men stuffed their shirts with false bosoms, and the girls borrowed codpieces that they likewise stuffed out appropriately. As ale was a part of the feast, the barriers of propriety were often broken. There was much kissing, many speeches were full of references to taboo subjects, and those known to be lovers were teased.

All of these events were joyful expressions of thankfulness following the safe completion of the harvest. This gratitude was extended both to the spirit of the fields and to the mowers themselves, who were figures of some power. Often the mowers were itinerant workers, who traveled in bands from farm to farm, always certain of work. In some areas, a Harvest

A harvest supper, where the farmer rewarded the hardworking mowers and their families with a grand feast.

Lord or King of the Mowers was elected from among them. He commanded great respect, as he negotiated wages and hours for his fellow reapers. His word was law in the fields; he regulated the pace of the work, disciplined slackers, and determined break times during which tools could be sharpened. In an earlier time, this role probably included priestly functions, such as choosing a suitable sacrifice and conducting rituals designed to ensure a successful harvest.

Lammas Tide

In Celtic countries, the Harvest Home festival was also called *Lammas*, an Anglo-Saxon word that means "Loaf Mass" or "bread feast." The name derives from the first loaves baked after harvest. It was said that if the first loaf came out of the oven well, all that followed through the year would be well baked and wholesome. In later times, these first loaves were consecrated in church.

In more ancient times, Lammas was known as *Lughnasadh*, a day dedicated to the Celtic god Lugh, a figure similar to the Roman god Mercury, master of crafts and skills, travelers, and commerce. Lugh was a solar deity (his name means "light" or "shining") and the consort of the goddess of abundance. Thus his festival was dedicated to the harvesting of wild fruits and the celebration of life itself. In many areas a maiden was selected, dressed in white garments, and seated beside a local shrine or sacred spot. People decorated the shrine, and processions formed to bring the first fruits of the wildwood to her. Gifts of blackberries, sloes, acorns, and crab apples were piled into her lap. Afterward, there was a general dance and a festive procession home. The white-clad maiden is almost certainly related to the May Queen and the Lady of Summer, one of the facets of the Goddess representing the qualities of the year.

A Lammas tradition that survived into the nineteenth century was a series of processions around pasture lands. Originally, these processions were for marking the boundaries of pastures owned in common by villagers. After common lands had been divided, the custom continued in a ceremonial way. All gates dividing parcels of land were left open so that horsemen decked in their best clothes could make the circuit. Feasts were held at various farms or at an inn in town where a special Lammas ale was brewed.

In Scotland, cowherders in the Lothians held high festival at Lammas tide. They collected stones and

The mystical sun-boat rises above New Grange, Ireland, and Chaco Canyon, New Mexico, in this painting by Hue Walker.

sods from the pastures to build a tower on a high point of land. Then on Lammas Day they came out dressed in their best clothes, rode their horses around the pasture boundaries, and held footraces and a feast near the tower. By custom, the cowherders in one area conducted raids on the towers built by other groups of cow herders. They would attack a nearby tower in a general melee, blowing on cow-horn bugles and trying to seize and tear down the "castle" of their neighbors. The battles were good humored, and any injuries were washed away by the ale feast that followed. These mock battles may derive from an older Celtic custom that decreed that a man had jurisdiction as far as his voice could carry from the top of the dunghill in his yard!

Corn Mothers and Corn Dances

Europe was not the only place where corn dolls were used to represent the spirit of the harvested grain. Among the people of ancient Peru, it was customary to take the most fruitful portion of the maize and dress it in rich garments. This effigy, called the Mother of the Maize, was held in great veneration.

The Peruvians shared a belief common throughout the Americas that all useful plants were animated by a divine being who caused their growth. Thus corn had its Maize Mother (*Zara-mama*), quinoa its Quinoa Mother (*Quinoa-mama*); cocoa its Cocoa Mother (*Coca-mama*), potato its Potato Mother (*Axo-mama*), and so on. Effigies of these divinities were constructed from the leaves and sheaves of the plants in question and dressed in women's clothes. The figures were female as they were considered to be mothers who generated and gave birth to the crops.

Corn, or maize, was a staple food among many Native American groups. Among the Iroquois of New York State, corn, beans, and squash are referred to as the "three sisters" and are always mentioned in the same breath. Myths that tell of the disappearance and return of the Corn Maiden or Mother are told among many of the maize-growing peoples, some strongly reminiscent of the Greek myth of the abduction of Kore or Persephone. Ceremonial dances that celebrate the planting, growth, and harvesting of maize are widely performed, especially in the Southwest and in the New Mexican pueblos (villages).

The Pueblo Green Corn Dance retains fragments of much older ceremonies that were enacted secretly in the underground ritual houses known as kivas. The dances are actually elaborate ceremonies designed to honor and encourage the crops, the rainbow, the rain clouds, and the corn itself, as well as to celebrate the harvest. The dances begin with the entrance of the koshare, who impersonates the ancestral spirits. This opening is followed by an enactment of a defense of the crops against invaders. Finally the men and women of the summer and winter kivas begin a dance that continues until sunset. A men's chorus drums and chants in shifting rhythms to accompany them, while the women follow slightly behind the trotting men in a huge double circle, long double lines, or small circles consisting of one or two couples. Similar dances are performed by the Shawnee, Cherokee, Creek, Yuchi, and Iroquois peoples. Many of these dances follow a serpentine or spiral course with gestures that emulate sowing.

A spirit dancer brings light to San Ildefonso Pueblo, New Mexico. (Painting by Chris Castle)

During the time of the corn dances, many stories are told concerning the origins of corn and its life-preserving properties. The Penobscot tell how the First Mother provided food for her starving offspring by commanding her husband and sons to kill her and spread her flesh on the earth. Seven moons after they did so, they visited the spot where the First Mother had fallen and found tall, green tasseled plants growing from the earth. This was said to be the first corn, grown from the Corn Mother's flesh to feed her children.

A gruesome Abnaki myth tells a slightly different story. In it, a beautiful, golden-haired woman appears to a lonely and hungry man. At first, she will not allow him to touch her; rather, she instructs him to burn a patch of ground. Then, promising that if he obeys her, she will be with him forever, she tells the man to kill her and drag her body across the burned patch. The man does as he is told, and soon a plant springs up where the woman's body had touched the ground. Looking closely, he sees the bright golden hair of the woman shining between the leaves of the plant and understands that she has kept her promise through the gift of the corn. Stories of this kind emphasize the sacrifice and dedication necessary to successfully harvest the land, as well as the eternal bond between the earth and those who reap its goodness.

The Soul of the Rice

The belief that a staple crop such as corn possessed a divine spirit was not limited to Europe and the Americas. In the Far East, among the Malay and Dyak people of Indonesia, rice plants were traditionally believed to be animated by a vital spark, similar to the human soul. Likewise, the propagation, growth, maturation, and death of rice plants was seen to correspond to the human life cycle. Thus Indonesian farmers treated the plants with deference and consideration. They behaved toward growing rice as they would toward a pregnant woman, abstaining from making loud noises in the field lest they frighten the soul of the rice and cause it to miscarry. For the same reason, they never spoke of death or demons in the rice fields and fed the growing rice with foods believed to be wholesome to pregnant women. When the rice ears were just beginning to form, women went through the fields feeding the plants with rice pap as if they were human babies.

This belief also affected the harvesting of rice. Every precaution was taken to make the operation as painless to the rice as possible. Traditionally, the reaping of seed rice was done with small knives, the blades hidden in the reapers' hands. This ensured that the rice spirit would know nothing of its fate until the last moment, when the head of the plant was swept off. The reapers at work in the fields even employed a special form of speech, which, it was believed, the rice spirit could not understand, so that the plant had no warning of what was about to happen.

Among the peoples who personified rice in this way, the Kayans of Central Borneo used a number of curious devices to capture the soul of the rice. These included a spatula, a miniature ladder, and a basket containing hooks, thorns, and cords. A priestess would use the spatula to urge the soul of the rice down the little ladder into the basket, where it would be captured by the hooks, the thorn, and the cord. Thus imprisoned, the rice soul was carried with the harvest to the rice granary.

In order to ensure a good harvest for the following year, the Kayans also believed that it was necessary to capture the soul of every single grain of rice, including recovering any part of the soul that might have fallen to the earth or been eaten by deer, apes, and pigs. To this end, instruments of various sorts were used by priests, such as a bamboo vessel with four hooks made from the wood of a fruit tree. Any missing

Among the native people of Bali, Indonesia, the soul of the rice fields was honored every year.

portion of the rice soul was drawn into the vessel, which was then hung up in the house. Every time a Kayan housewife fetched rice from the granary she was careful to propitiate the soul of the rice, lest the rice should be angry at being robbed of its substance.

The need to secure the soul of the rice is also part of the beliefs of the Karen people of Burma. When a rice field failed to flourish, it was believed that the soul of the rice had somehow left the field. If the soul could not be called back, the crop would fail, so the following song was sung to call back the soul (kelah) of the rice:

Come, O Rice-kelah, come!
Come to the field.
Come to the rice...
Come from the West,
Come from the East.
From the throat of the bird,
From the maw of the ape,
From the throat of the elephant...
O Rice-kelah, come to the rice.

The Rice Child

The anthropologist Edward B. Taylor witnessed a ceremony for cutting and bringing home the rice soul in the Malay Peninsula in 1897. First the sheaf that was to serve as the mother of the rice soul was identified by studying the markings or shape of the ears. Then an aged sorceress solemnly cut from this sheaf a bundle of seven ears, which she anointed with oil, tied together with multicolored thread, and cleansed with incense. Having wrapped the ears in a white cloth, she deposited them in an oval-shaped basket. These seven ears represented the infant soul of the rice and the little basket its cradle, a practice reminiscent of the making of Bride Oggs in Scotland.

The infant rice soul was carried home to the farmer's house by another woman, who held up an umbrella to screen it from the hot rays of the sun. At the house the rice child was welcomed by the women of the family and laid, cradle and all, on a new sleeping mat with pillows at the head. For three days, the farmer's wife observed various rules of taboo, much as she would after the birth of a real child.

Similar care was extended to the mother of the rice child, the sheaf from whose body it had been taken. This sheaf, which remained standing in the field after the rice soul had been carried home and put to bed, was treated as a new mother. It was allowed to "rest" for three days, after which it was reaped by the farmer's wife, who carried it back to the house, threshed it, and mixed it with the rice soul. The farmer then took the mixture and its basket and deposited both in the great circular rice bin used by the Malays. Care was taken to mix grains from the rice soul with the seed that was to be sown the following year.

The harvested rice in Bali, Indonesia, is perceived as an expression of the gods of the earth.

Churches throughout the West are decorated with flowers and sheaves of corn at harvest time.

In some Indonesian cultures, the life cycle of the rice plant also included marriage. In Java, as recently as the nineteenth century, a ritual wedding between the male and female spirits of the rice was celebrated as part of the harvest. Before the reapers began to cut the rice, a priest picked out a number of ears, which were tied together, smeared with ointment, and adorned with flowers. Thus decked out, the ears were called the Rice Bride and Bridegroom, and their wedding feast was celebrated, after which the cutting of the rice began immediately. Later, when the rice had been harvested, a bridal chamber was partitioned off in the barn and furnished with a new mat, a lamp, and various household articles. Sheaves of rice, to represent the wedding guests, were placed beside the Rice Bride and Groom. Only after the rice couple was settled could the harvest be housed in the barn. For forty days after the rice had been placed in the barn, no one could enter for fear of disturbing the newly wedded pair. Similar customs still take place in Bali.

Remembering the Sacred Year

With the arrival of mechanized farming, the old customs connected with the harvest have faded away in many parts of the world. In Britain and Northern Europe, they have been absorbed, as were so many initially pagan practices, into the customs of the Christian Church. The modern tradition of harvest festivals, held in local churches to the accompaniment of hymns like "We Plow the Fields and Scatter" and "Come Ye Thankful People Come," and with samples of local produce piled up around the altar, date only from the nineteenth century, when reformers strove to drive out any lingering vestiges of an older spirit.

Despite such efforts, the traditions of the harvest have not died out entirely, and around the world, the events celebrated around the time of the Summer Solstice and in the months leading up to the harvest remind us of the way things were. Though we may no longer feel the need to placate the gods or goddesses of the sun, such observances are as important now as they ever were. Honoring the patterns of the seasonal round keeps us in touch with our environment and the natural world, which we neglect to our loss.

Making a Corn Doll

Making a corn doll brings the spirit of the harvest into the home. The simplest method is to gather a small sheaf of corn stalks and bind them together around the middle with red wool or ribbon (red is a sacred color in many lands) so that the top and bottom fan out. Then create a simple "dress" for the doll from a handkerchief.

A more elaborate woven doll requires longer stems of either corn or wheat. Strip any leaves from the stems and wrap the stems in a damp cloth until they are pliable. Then take five stems and tie them together in the middle. Weave them as follows: cross straw one over straws two and three; then cross the straw immediately to the left of straw one over the next two straws, so that straw three crosses over straws one and four, and straw four crosses over straws three and five. Continue until you have built up a roughly square-shaped form.

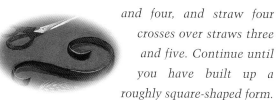

Dress the doll in scraps of cloth or ribbons and hang it from the ceiling or mantelpiece. Infuse the doll with the magic of the harvest by making it outdoors, perhaps while retelling a harvest story or recounting a harvest tradition that you remember or have learned about in this book. You might also make up a chant to sing while making the corn doll, or use the one given here:

Corn stooks and barley
Make the Maiden bonny;
Corn rows and cockle-flowers
Tied with red ribbon,
Draw down blessings
On the one who weaves.

The Ripe and Bearded Barley

Come out, 'tis now September,
The hunter's moon's begun,
And through the wheaten stubble
We hear the frequent gun.
The leaves are turning yellow,
And fading into red,
While the ripe and bearded barley
Is hanging down its head.

ANON

A Harvest Supper

Even if you don't live on a farm and have never raised a reaping hook, why not hold your own Harvest Home supper? This tradition, whether celebrated on Thanksgiving Day as in the United States or at any other time in the late summer or fall, gives us the opportunity to express gratitude for the riches that come our way.

WHEAT-SHEAF BREAD

Baking a loaf of bread shaped like a wheat sheaf is a great way to remind yourself and your guests of the real reason for a harvest celebration.

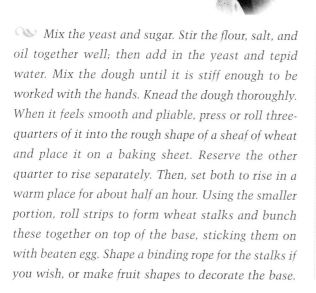

1 lb or 500 g of flour
1 tsp salt
1 oz or 25 g of fresh yeast
1 oz or 25 g of sugar
½ pt of tepid water or stock
1 tbsp vegetable oil
1–2 beaten eggs for glaze

 Mix the yeast and sugar. Stir the flour, salt, and oil together well; then add in the yeast and tepid water. Mix the dough until it is stiff enough to be worked with the hands. Knead the dough thoroughly. When it feels smooth and pliable, press or roll three-quarters of it into the rough shape of a sheaf of wheat and place it on a baking sheet. Reserve the other quarter to rise separately. Then, set both to rise in a warm place for about half an hour. Using the smaller portion, roll strips to form wheat stalks and bunch these together on top of the base, sticking them on with beaten egg. Shape a binding rope for the stalks if you wish, or make fruit shapes to decorate the base.

Keep in mind as you form the dough that the shape will change as the dough rises. Lightly cover the loaf with oiled plastic wrap (clingfilm) and a cloth and allow it to rise for a further 15 minutes. Then brush the loaf with beaten egg and sprinkle it with wheat grains or oats. Bake at 425° (U.K. Gas Mark 7) for 10 minutes; then reduce the heat to 375° and bake for 20 to 25 minutes more. Check to see if the loaf is done by tapping the underside with a knife. If it sounds hollow, it's ready. If not, bake for another 5 minutes.

DAMSON AND APPLE TANSEY

This fruit dessert is an adaptation of a fifteenth-century recipe traditionally served at harvest feasts.

8 oz or 225 g of very ripe damsons (or ripe dark plums)
8 oz or 225 g of cooking apples
2 oz or 50 g of butter
2–3 oz or 50–75 g superfine (caster) sugar
2 beaten egg yolks
4 tsp of fresh bread crumbs
¼ pt or 50ml of heavy cream (double cream)
1 tsp orange juice

 Wash the apples and damsons, core, and slice them. Melt the butter in a saucepan with 2–3 oz (60 ml) water. Add the fruit and boil until soft. Press the fruit through a sieve and put the puree back into the pan. While still off the heat, stir in enough sugar to bring out the taste. Blend in the beaten egg yolks and breadcrumbs. Stir over a low heat until the mixture thickens. Allow it to cool. Whisk the cream lightly and fold it into the puree. Sharpen the flavor with the orange juice and spoon into individual serving glasses.

Chapter Six

DAYS OF THE SUN:
A Calendar of Festivals and Celebrations

Rise, and put on your Foliage, and be seene

To come forth, like the Spring-time, fresh and greene;

And sweet as Flora. Take no care

For Jewels for your Gowne, or Haire.

Feare not; the leaves will strew

Gemms in abundance upon you...

Few Beads are best, when once

we goe a Maying.

"CORINNA'S GOING A MAYING," ROBERT HERRICK

The Summer Solstice has always been a time for celebrations; many community festivals and fairs still take place around this time. Attending such events is a wonderful way to enter into the spirit of the solstice. In this chapter, you will find accounts of solstice events that still flourish between May and September—some, perhaps, near to where you live or in a place to which you might travel—as well as additional suggestions for creating your own summer celebrations. Whether you wish to light a fire, make a corn doll, jump a bonfire, or set candles in the windows of your home to honor the Midsummer sun, you will find something here to help you participate personally in the festivities of the season.

May

May Day is celebrated throughout the world. In Greece, children set out early in the morning to seek the first swallow of spring. After they have seen the bird, they go from house to house singing songs to bring word of the return of spring. They are generally rewarded with special cakes, nuts, and fruit, gathered for the occasion.

In Italy, where May Day celebrations were once devoted to the goddess Flora, a general holiday feeling still exists, with people singing in the streets and decorating their houses and churches with flowers. Boys traditionally serenade their sweethearts on this day, as they would have done in Roman times.

In Switzerland, Germany, and the Czech Republic, young men plant May trees outside the windows of their sweethearts, decorating them with fruits and blossoms, hoping in this way to win the favor of the intended girl.

Throughout the French countryside, processions in honor of the Virgin Mary take place, often led by a May Queen, selected from among the local village girls. Cows are herded through the streets, their tails decorated with flowers and ribbons. It is considered good luck to drink fresh milk, still warm from the animal, the first thing on May Day morning.

In the United States, May Day has never been celebrated with the same enthusiasm as in Europe. The Puritan Fathers frowned on such activities and discouraged their followers from retaining the old ways. Despite this early suppression, the traditions did continue, and to this day, you can see May Day celebrations complete with a Maypole and May Queen in towns and on college campuses across the country. There is a lovely tradition in some places; children hang paper baskets filled with flowers from the door knobs of houses. They ring the doorbell and run off, leaving the flowers as a surprise.

In Hawaii, May Day is also Lei Day, and flowered leis are exchanged between friends. To this day a Lei Queen is chosen from among the young women of the Islands, proving that Maytime traditions are alive and well even in remote parts of the world.

But it is in Britain that we find the strongest traditions relating to the celebration of May. In the southwest corner of the island, the little town of Padstow, in Cornwall, holds one of the most spectacular May Day festivals to be seen anywhere. The celebration begins at midnight on April 30th with the singing of the "May Night Song":

Unite, unite, let us all unite,
For Summer is a-come today
And wither we are going we all will unite
On the merry morning of May.

The young men of Padstow they might if they wold,
For Summer is a-come unto day.
They might ha' built a ship and gilded her with gold.
On the merry morning of May

The maidens of Padstow they might if they wold,
For Summer is a-come unto day.

The magical 'Oss leads the way at the Padstow festival in Cornwall, U.K.

of black fabric hanging down to the ground. The dancer's head emerges from the dark circle, covered by a strange pointed mask painted in the sacred colors of red, white, and black. At one time the skirt was heavily tarred, and the 'Oss would grab any passing young woman and draw her under his skirts, from which she emerged red faced, giggling, and marked with streaks of black—a sure sign of fertility, it was believed. Nowadays, the 'Oss is led through the streets by a "teaser," a raucous clown who trades insults and jokes with everyone he passes.

The dancing continues through the night and into the next day, the "May Night Song" giving way to the "Morning Song" of May Day itself. Several of the verses contain blanks into which the names of local figures are inserted at will, often to great hilarity. Why not try putting in some names of your own?

They might have made a garland of the white rose
and the red
On the merry morning of May.

Up Merry Spring, and up the merry ring,
For Summer is a-come unto day.
How happy are those little birds that merrily do sing
On the merry morning of May.

After the singing, a strange procession wends its way through the streets to the beat of several large drums, led by a character known as the 'Oss (horse). The dancer who portrays this creature has to be very strong, as he must support a costume consisting of a wide black disk of material stretched over a wooden frame, with a skirt

Unite, unite, and it's all how white,
For Summer is a-come in to-day,

And whither we are going we will all unite
In the merry morning of May.

I warn you young men every one
To go to the greenwood and fetch your May home.

Arise, Master _____ and joy you betide,
And bright is your bride that lies by your side.

Arise, Mistress _____ and gold be your ring
And give us a cup of ale that merrier we may sing.

With the merry sing and now joyful spring,
How happy are the birds that merrily do sing.

Arise, Master _____ with your sword by your side,
Your steed is in stable awaiting you to ride.

Arise, Master _____ and reach me your hand,
And you shall have a lovely lass with a thousand
*   pounds in hand.*

Arise, Master _____ for I know you well and fine,
You've a shilling in your purse, I wish it were in mine.

Arise, Miss _____ and strew all your flowers,
It is but a little while since we strewed ours.

With the merry sing and now joyful spring,
How happy are the birds that merrily do sing.

Arise, Miss _____ from out of your bed,
Your chamber shall be spread with the white rose
*   and red.*

Arise, Miss _____ all in your smock of silk,
And all your body under as white as any milk.

Where are the young men that now here should dance?
Some they are in England and some are in France.

Where are the maidens that now here should sing?
They are all in the meadows a flower gathering.

For the merry sing now the joyful spring,
How happy are the birds that merrily do sing.

The young men of Padstow they might if they wold,
They might ha' built a ship and gilded her with gold.

The maidens of Padstow they might if they wold,
They have made a garland and gilded it with gold.

Now fare you well and we wish you good cheer,
We will come no more unto your house until
*   another year.*

For the merry sing now the joyful spring,
How happy are the birds that merrily do sing.

Around midday, the proceedings take on a different rhythm; the heartbeat of the drums is stilled, and everyone takes up a new song, unaccompanied. In it, we hear of St. George, a familiar figure in English folk custom. References to "the French dogs" suggest that the original song dated from one of the medieval wars between England and France.

Awake St. George, our English knight O,
For summer is a come, and winter is a go.
Where is St. George and where is he O?
He's down in his long boat upon the salt sea O.
For to fetch summer home, summer and May O,
For summer is a come and winter is a go.

Where are the French dogs that make such
*   boast O?*
They shall eat the goose feathers and we'll eat the
*   roast O.*
Thou mightst ha' shown a knavish face, or tarried
*   at home O,*
But thou shall be a cuckold and wear the horns O.

Up flies the kite, down falls the lark O,
Aunt Ursula Birdwood, she had an old ewe.
Aunt Ursula Birdwood, she had an old ewe,
And she died in her own park long ago.

Just who Aunt Ursula Birdwood may be is long forgotten, though it is safe to assume that she was either a local figure of some importance or a familiar name for the "wise woman" who represents the archetype of natural feminine wisdom underlying this season of fertility. Thus, though the origins of the Padstow celebration are lost in time, they still continue, adapted to modern days.

In Oxfordshire, in the little village of Charlton-on-Otmoor, a service is held in the local parish church on the morning of May 1. A figure made up of greenery, representing the vital energy of May, sits on top of the screen behind the altar. After the service, a procession begins, in which the May Queen and May Day dancers perform ancient steps.

Nearby, also on May Day morning, Magdalen College, Oxford, continues what is in all probability a medieval tradition. At six in the morning, the college choir sings carols from the top of Magdalen Tower, welcoming the newly risen sun. After the singing, Morris dancers lead a procession through the streets. Many Oxford students turn out, participating in the festivities by jumping into the River Cherwell that runs beneath Magdalen Bridge.

On the Isle of Man, the May Day festival of Laa Boaldyn is celebrated with full ritual panoply. On May Eve, the people go up onto the mountains and set fire to the gorse to frighten away the fairy folk. Then, on May Day morning itself, they welcome in the festival with a loud blowing of horns, again with the aim of driving away fairies. The May Queen, mounted on a horse, is led into the village, attended by some twenty maidens and an equal number of boys led by a captain, who form the Queen's bodyguard. Folklorist Eleanor Hull, quoting from a manuscript description of Manx customs, adds the following:

In opposition to her [the Queen of May] is the Queen of Winter, a man dressed in woman's clothes, with woolen hood, fur tippets, and laden with the heaviest and warmest habits, one upon the other. In the same manner are her attendants dressed, and she also has a captain and troop for her defense. Being thus equipped as proper emblems of the Beauty of Spring and the Deformity of Winter, the two parties set forth from their respective quarters, the one preceded by violins and flutes, the other with the rough music of tongs and cleavers. Both parties march till they meet on a common, where their followers engage in a mock battle.

William Holman Hunt's painting shows choristers on the tower of Magdalen College, Oxford, U.K. welcoming the May morning.

If the forces of the Queen of Winter get the upper hand and succeed in taking the Queen of May prisoner, she has to be ransomed for a sum that will pay the expenses of the day; after which, Winter and her attendants retire to a barn to amuse themselves while the others dance on the green. They conclude the evening with a feast, the Queen at one table with her maids, the captain with his troop at another. There are seldom less than fifty or sixty at each board.

It is easy to see in this annual event a version of the ancient ritual struggle between the representatives of Summer and Winter.

On the first Saturday of May, the Gawthorpe May Festival takes place at Ossett in Yorkshire. In mid-afternoon, a procession carrying a Maypole begins from Gawthorpe Village and progresses to Ossett Market Place. Led by the May Queen and her six maids of honor, all on horseback and led by a band, the parade also includes a hundred other riders. Once the Maypole is set up, celebrations and dancing begins.

The May celebration in Helston, Cornwall, is held on May 8th. At noon, a procession leaves the Guildhall and winds in and out of many of the larger buildings and through the crowd, to the accompaniment of the famous "Floral Day Song." Some believe that this carol honors Flora, the Roman goddess of spring, but many local people insist that its proper name is the Furry song, not the Floral song. Perhaps the real explanation is that *Furry* is a corruption of "Fairy" and that the song and the dance suggested by its lyrics honor the inhabitants of the Otherworld. Traditionally, musicians in the Helston Silver Band who play "The Furry Day Carol" learn the music from others who have played it, never from written notes.

Robin Hood and Little John
Are both gone to the fair O
And we will go to the merry Greenwood
To see what they do there O
And for to chase
To chase the buck and the doe.

Chorus:
Hal-an-tow, Jolly Rumble O
We were up long before the day O
To welcome in the Summer
To welcome in the May O
For Summer it is a-comin in
And Winter's gone away O!

Where are those Spaniards
That make so great a boast O
They shall eat the grey goose feather
And we will eat the roast O
In every land O
The land where're we go.

Morris dancers perform a traditional show for the public at Stratford-upon-Avon, U.K.

(Chorus)

As for the good knight St. George
St. George he was a knight O
Of all the knights in Christendom
St. George he was the right O
In every land O
The land where're we go.

(Chorus)

God bless Aunt Mary Moses
And all her power and might O
And send us peace in Merry England
Both day and night O
And sends us peace in Merry England
Both now and ever more O.

(Chorus)

As this song reminds us, in many parts of Britain, Robin Hood, the bold outlaw of Sherwood Forest, represents the Lord of the May, as St. George represents the triumph of light over darkness. The words "Hal-an-tow" in the refrain are probably a corruption of "heel and toe" and refer to dance steps that once accompanied the song. Aunt Mary Moses seems to be an archetypal figure similar to Aunt Ursula Birdwood in the Padstow "May Night Song." The Spanish boast refers to the Armada of 1588, which was defeated, according to tradition, because the witches of England raised a storm that drove the ships onto the rocks.

In Castleton, Derbyshire, a wonderful celebration known as the Garland King Day takes place on May 29th. This event is said to celebrate the escape of King Charles II from the Roundheads (Puritans). In the early morning, a procession, including a man dressed as the Merry Monarch and carrying a garland, rides through the village. When it arrives at the Market Square, Maypole dancing begins and continues for the day.

Older accounts of the Castleton celebration point to a far more ancient time, when the May Day games included the ritual beheading of the Summer Lord. On May 29th a huge bell-shaped garland is constructed, which is worn over the head of a chosen King. He is then led in procession through the streets on horseback. On reaching the local church the framework of greenery and flowers is hooked up to a winch that then hauls it to the top of the tower, where it is left to swing in the wind until the elements gradually demolish it. At one time, it was probably a sacrificial victim whose body—or head—was carried aloft, maybe to swing from the topmost branches of a tree. Such things link more recent folk traditions with a far older time, when the propitiation of the gods of nature was a far more serious business.

In your own celebrations of May, you can adapt any of the traditions above to suit your needs or those of your community. These traditions have always changed to fit circumstances; perhaps that is why they have survived and evolved over the years. Creating your own celebration is an important way of keeping these ancient ways alive.

Your May celebration need not be elaborate. You might, for example, use the day to spring clean your home. Do so in a more ritual fashion than usual, thinking about everything that is no longer necessary in your life, including old habits and patterns of thinking, that can be swept out along with the dust and the rubbish that clutters your home. Clearing away old items will allow you to bring in the new.

If you have a garden, planting flowers, herbs, or vegetables can also be an important and practical way of acknowledging the power of spring. Even if you do no more than plant a new window box or houseplant, or bring fresh flowers into your home or workplace, you will have participated in the dance of spring and responded to the urgent energy of Maytime.

June

June brings the Summer Solstice and the beginning of summer proper. It is the time of many fascinating celebrations and events around the world.

Those fortunate enough to be at Chaco Canyon, New Mexico, on the day of the Summer Solstice will be able to see the spectacular lighting of the petroglyph known as the Sun Dagger by the first rays of the risen sun. A single blade of light, called the Sun Dagger, bisects the center of a spiral carved on the rock face of the 450-foot-high Fajada Butte (see page 135). The Anasazi people, who lived in this area until the fourteenth century, used this carving to determine the best time to plant and harvest and to record the passage of time.

In Baja California, at the San Carlos Mesa, a beam of sunlight strikes the rock face next to a petroglyph of a native house exactly at noon on the day of the solstice. After approximately eleven minutes, the light moves across to the house and finally dwindles to a spot that appears to enter the door of the building and vanish. For the Tipai people who dwelled in the area, this site was a profound statement of the seasonal pattern. The entry of the sun into its house, which resembled those in which the Tipai lived, offered them reassurance of the continued blessing of the light.

Brimfield, Illinois, puts on a spectacular Old English Faire in late June at the Jubilee College Park. A rustic marketplace, complete with strolling medieval players and all kinds of games and contests, mimics the atmosphere of a medieval European fair. Many other such fairs are held in towns and villages throughout the United States. Check with your local town hall or cultural center, or the internet, for further information.

In France, at Chartres Cathedral outside Paris, the chairs that normally cover the great labyrinth are removed on Midsummer Eve. This is a wonderful opportunity to walk this sacred pattern, which people believe echoes the dance of the Midsummer sun. Elsewhere in France, many Midsummer celebrations still take place. Familiar traditions such as giant bonfires, dancing through the night, and couples jumping over the ashes of the fires to ensure fertility are part of these observances. Here is a description of the Midsummer customs of a cluster of villages around Munster and St. Jean in the Alsace region:

Sitting in a circle in the middle of a river of red roses, women and girls are busy sewing the flowers onto broad-brimmed hats in the small village courtyard. After pinching the stems, they fix the roses in little bunches of four or five until the whole of the hat is covered with them. The mothers keep an eye on what the girls are doing because these strange hats are to be worn by their sons that same evening when they jump over the fire. It is, in fact, the moisture in the middle of the roses that provides a cool area round the head and protects the boys from the flames and the intense heat of the bonfire.

As nightfall approaches, a procession forms, and the whole village makes its way to the fire, which has been laid on a nearby hill but not yet lit. The village children carry torches, which they light and then run off with down the hill, whirling them around their heads as they go. Having made a complete circuit of the hill, the children return to the fire and set the huge mound of dry brushwood and vines alight. As the flames die down, the boys put on their rose-bedecked hats, cover their faces with scarves, and jump across the fire, while the girls remain as near as possible to the embers.

When the ceremony is over, everyone descends to the village square and begins a circling dance in front of the town hall, turning always in a sunwise direction to imitate the sun's movement through the heavens.

Nearby, in villages of the Thurn and Thann valleys, towers up to a hundred feet high are built and set on fire. Their light can be seen for miles from the hilltops, much as it was centuries ago.

In Ireland, an ancient custom has found new celebrants. People of many beliefs have started gathering at the hill of Tara in the Boyne Valley to watch the Midsummer sunrise. Tara is one of the most sacred sites in Ireland, the seat of the ancient High Kings and the sacred center of the country. Modern-day Druids gather about the standing stone, known as the Lia Fail, or the Stone of Destiny, that rises from the center of the hill. Staffs decorated with blossom and ribbons are laid around the stone on Midsummer Day.

On the night and day of the solstice, June 20th and 21st, a celebration organized by the modern Druid Orders takes place at Parliament Hill Fields in London. People begin to gather on Midsummer Eve for a midnight vigil, sometimes walking to the nearby site believed to be the tomb of the Celtic Queen Boudicca. In the predawn darkness, a procession to greet the dawn begins. Various rituals are enacted, including one in which a senior Druid calls out: "Is it Peace?"—presumably a reference to some ancient war. A statement of Druid aims follows. The ancient Celtic trumpet known as the dord is sounded to greet the sun, followed by a performance of music and poetry.

On Midsummer Day, June 22nd, the Druid Orders' most important ceremony takes place at Stonehenge in Wiltshire. Druids gather on Midsummer Eve and keep watch until sunrise, at which time they conduct a ritual by the altar stone. Afterward there are readings, and the ancient horn is sounded to the four directions

A spectacular sunset over
Fajada Butte, Chaco Canyon,
New Mexico, U.S.A.

of the compass. Despite clashes with demonstrators and police in recent years, this ancient tradition survives and may still be seen from outside a perimeter fence. One example of a modern song, written by Caitlín Matthews for a contemporary Druid Order, appears printed on page 34. (For more information about Druidry, contact The Secretary, Order of Bards, Ovates and Druids, P.O. Box 1333, Lewes, East Sussex, BN7 1DX, United Kingdom. Or log on to their website at www.druidry.org.)

At Kithill, on the Devon/Cornwall border, another great bonfire, perhaps the largest in Britain, is lit as the last rays of the sun strike across the moorland on Midsummer Eve. A brief ritual, featuring a Lady of the Flowers and a Master of Ceremonies, is enacted in Cornish. In translation, the dialog goes as follows:

Master of Ceremonies: According to the custom of our ancestors, behold us making our Midsummer Fire on this night.
Now set the pyre
At once on fire
Let flame aspire
In God's high name!

The Lady of the Flowers comes forward and casts bunches of herbs, both beneficial and poisonous, into the fire, while saying:

In one bunch together bound
Flowers for burning here are found
Both good and ill
Thousandfold let good seed spring
Wicked weeds fast withering
Let this fire kill!

Many ways to celebrate Midsummer have been mentioned in previous chapters. In addition, you might transform your garden into a fairy place by hanging lanterns in the trees and putting tea lights in glasses all through the garden. When night falls, the twinkling lights will create an enchanted atmosphere to meet, eat, and tell stories.

Another perfect way to celebrate is getting together with a few friends to read aloud from *A Midsummer Night's Dream*, or to attend one of the many outdoor productions of the play that take place at summer Shakespeare festivals.

Above all, Midsummer is a night for dreams. So, why not sleep out under the stars on this special night? Think about a question, your hopes, or fears as you

To this day Druids gather at Stonehenge, Wiltshire, to celebrate the Midsummer Solstice.

drift off and ask that they be answered through your dreams, perhaps even by the fairies.

Possibly the oldest surviving Midsummer fire ceremony in Britain takes place on the 4th of July at Whalton, in Northumberland. It is known as the Baal Fire, a name that probably derives from the Celtic sun god *Bel* (bright) or possibly from the Saxon word *bael* (fire). Carloads of gorse and other fuel are brought by cart to the edge of the village and carried by men to the accompaniment of the blowing of horns. The fire is then lit and dancing and singing take place around it throughout the night. The custom continues, but sadly fewer people attend every year.

July 4th, Independence Day, brings its own series of celebrations across the United States. Backyard barbecues, parades, speeches (including the reading of the Declaration of Independence), concerts, and firework displays take place all over the country.

This Fourth of July procession in New York echoes all the riotous joy of Midsummer festivals from times past.

Although these events are not traditionally connected to the solstice, they deserve mention here as an aspect of the lighthearted and joyful energy that accompanies this time of the year.

July in general brings many other outdoor festivals across the United States. At Bayou La Batre, Alabama, the annual blessing of the Shrimp Fleet takes place on the last Sunday in July. Barnsville, Pennsylvania, holds a Bavarian Summer Festival over the first two weeks of July, which reflects the spirit of the German Midsummer celebrations. Adams, Tennessee, holds a spirited Thresherman's Show in mid-July. The three-day festival includes demonstrations of old-time threshing, quilting, and corn-shelling, as well as buggy rides and a fiddle contest.

August/September

In Celtic countries, Lammas Day is celebrated on August 1st. Lammas began as the Celtic festival of Lughnasadh, which marked the gathering together of the tribes at the height of summer. The concerns of the hay harvest were mostly behind, and the prospect of the wheat and barley harvests was imminent. This was a time for showing off the speed of one's horses and competing in contests of skill and strength. It was also a time for arranging marriages, since young people would exhibit their qualities at this festival and form natural attachments, which their parents might, or might not, think suitable. Marriages were either love matches or arranged, with the interests of the clan at stake; young people of equal status were matched together. At Lughnasadh, trial marriages were entered into. Thrusting their hands through a holed stone, the couple would promise to live together for a year and a day, and to part after that time if either partner did not measure up to expectations.

Today Lammas Fairs take place all over Europe, and countless harvest festivals are organized throughout the British Isles and in parts of North America. They vary greatly between church-organized parades and intensely mystical, pagan-inspired events. Whatever the sponsorship, Lammas Fairs are occasions for fun, games, dancing , singing, and storytelling.

In South Queensferry, West Lothian, Scotland, the Burryman's Parade takes place during the second week of August. The parade and fair date back to a charter issued by Charles I in 1639. In addition to the traditional sports, games, dances, processions, and the crowning of the Harvest Queen, this festival features a unique and unusual custom. On the eve of the festival, a burly local man is wrapped in

Dancers holding ancient reindeer horns perform the Horn Dance at Abbots Bromley, Staffordshire, U.K.

flannels that are then covered with burrs. Dressed in this "burry-cloth," he is led from door to door to collect money for the fair. In all probability, the Burryman is a type of Green Man, a representative of the ancient spirit of nature.

In the traditional lunar Jewish calendar, the New Year falls on the first day of Tishrei (corresponding to September/October). Rosh Hashanah, as the New Year holiday is called, represents a new beginning. New clothes are always worn, and traditional greetings of "Shanah Tovah," or "Happy New Year," are exchanged. The themes of creation and renewal are central to the observance. Services are held in the

synagog with prayers, readings, and sacred songs celebrating the kingship of God and his power. A shofar, or sacred ram's horn, is blown ritually during the service. In earlier times a ritual cleansing was enacted at this time, during which people cast their sins from the past year into the waters. Rosh Hashanah begins a ten-day period of penitence and preparation that culminates in the solemn rites of Yom Kippur, the Day of Atonement, when observant Jews undertake a twenty-five hour fast.

The Jewish harvest festival known as Sukkot, the Feast of the Tabernacles, follows two weeks after the New Year holiday, on the 15th to the 22nd of Tishrei. In many synagogs and some homes, special tabernacles or "booths" are built of corn stalks and hung with gourds and other harvest symbols. Festive meals are held in these booths, with much singing, recalling the times when the Jewish people lived in such booths during their wanderings in the desert after the Exodus from Egypt.

One of the most spectacular English ceremonies to be seen during harvest time is the Abbots Bromley Horn Dance, which takes place on the Monday nearest to September 4th in Staffordshire. In the early morning, several sets of ancient reindeer horns are brought from the parish church, where they are stored during the year. The antlers are mounted onto deers' heads carried on poles. Some of the antlers are painted white; others have gold tips. Two musicians play a variety of folk tunes as dancers carrying the antlers perform a series of interwoven steps, first in a line, then in a circle. Splitting into two teams, they perform the Stag Dance, which imitates the clash of rutting stags. Advancing and retreating three times, the dancers meet and "fight," while other characters, including a Maid Marian, usually a man dressed as a woman, a Hobby Horse, a Fool, and a boy with a bow and arrow, clash sticks or bows in time to the music.

Finally the dancers form a line and continue on their way, repeating the pattern again and again throughout the day as they dance around the town.

The history of the dance is obscure; all that most people in the area remember is that it has been celebrated from "time immemorial." The horns themselves have been carbon dated to prehistoric times, and the dance steps have been passed from father to son down the generations. The elusive and mysterious tune that accompanies the dance is believed to be ancient but, once again, it has no definite origin. The characters who accompany the dancers are drawn from folklore traditions: Maid Marian comes from the Robin Hood myth, as perhaps, does the boy with the bow (he may also be Cupid). The Fool, like the trickster Puck, appears in traditional celebrations all over the world; while the Hobby Horse may be seen in May Day and Midsummer celebrations at Padstow and St. Ives.

In Hebron, Connecticut, a Harvest Fair takes place over four days in mid-September, with demonstrations of tractor pulling, oxen drawing, and various old-style harvest events and competitions. Similar fairs take place in many parts of the United States, with popular events at Fort Scott, Kansas, in early October, including demonstrations of bread making and displays of early pioneer harvesting methods. The towns of Sedgewick and Limon, Colorado, also have fall festivals that pay tribute to earlier times, with events such as tractor pulls and sack races. In Mitchell, South Dakota, at the annual Corn Palace Festival, over three thousand bushels of corn are used to decorate the venue. Demonstrations of corn-doll making also take place, and there is a carnival with fireworks.

Native American harvest festivals are also common across the United States. The Green Corn Festival is celebrated by (among others) the Creek, Cherokee, Seminole, Yuchi, and Iroquois peoples. During early September in New York State, a Green Corn Festival takes place that extends over four days and includes rites of thanksgiving for the harvest. Here you can witness the Great Feather Dance, the Women's Dance, and the Corn Dance. This last ceremony is addressed to the spirit of the corn, as represented by the three sisters: corn, beans, and squash, personified by three women appointed for life by tribal elders. Adorned with ribbons and shells, the women dance for as long as three hours.

A general thanksgiving ceremony is often held at this time in which old grudges are forgiven and forgotten. Over the first two days, people fast and cleanse themselves and their homes. They then drink a herbal concoction known as the Black Drink, which induces vomiting. After this purification, the first corn is harvested and tasted; dancing and singing follows.

In New Mexico, among the people of the pueblos, the Tablitas, or Saints' Day Dances, are held on August 4th to honor the harvest and bless the corn. The name *tablitas* refers to the high tablet crowns worn by the women who take part in the dance. These are usually decorated with eagle or parrot feathers and can be wonderfully elaborate. The dances held in Santo Domingo are the best preserved and are well worth a visit. Similar dances, also quite authentic, are held in San Felipe on May 1st. Nowadays there are signs of Christian influence in some of these dances, but thanks to the strength of tribal tradition, most have retained their authenticity. As always when visiting these dances, remember to show respect for the Native people whose guest you are.

The Alutiiq people of south coastal Alaska still gather in late fall to celebrate the end of the salmon fishing season and the berry harvest. Celebrations are held and dances and songs performed to address the spirits of the season. A Russian Orthodox priest witnessed one of these dances on Kodiac Island in 1804 and recorded his impressions:

Everyone comes: men, women, and young girls. The young men sit on benches, the women on the floor beneath the benches, each wife by the place occupied by her husband. The [older] men beat the drums and start to sing songs in honor of their ancestors and forefathers, remembering and reminiscing about how many baidara [large skin boats] they used to own, how many sea otters they had, and so on. Following the [older] men, everyone sings, while the [younger] men, dressed in their festive little hats and embroidered hoods, made especially for such occasions, each do their own dance. Holding rattles in their hands, they jump, crouch down, or sway their bodies from side to side, swinging the rattles in time. In these movements they represent their various hunting activities, for example, how a whaler spears a whale and then evades the animal, how a sea otter is chased, and so on. Later, they remove their festive caps and don various kinds of strange disguises and all sorts of masks. They dance [again] also to the accompaniment of songs and carrying rattles, either alone or in pairs, once again representing various actions.
(Trans. by Lydia Black.)

The present celebration has changed very little. If you are fortunate enough to be on Kodiac Island at this time, you can still witness this powerful celebration.

There are many ways to celebrate the harvest in addition to those mentioned in the previous chapter. For instance, you might arrange a "corn feast," featuring the different foods that can be made from corn: corn bread, tortillas, corn soup, and corn on the cob. Your house or table might be decorated corn stalks and corn dolls, gourds, pumpkins, and other harvest symbols.

Make your feast sacred by conducting a simple thanksgiving ritual either according to your own native or family tradition, or along these lines:

Designate someone to act as the celebrant. Spread a table with a freshly laundered white cloth and arrange some bread and other harvest produce on it, along with a cup of fresh water—if possible from a stream, river, or fountain, rather than from the tap (bottled spring water would do also). You should also decorate the table with candles, seasonal fruits, autumnal leaves, and flowers.

Gather your friends and family. The celebrant breaks the bread and pours a little of the water onto the earth outside the door, or on the hearth or windowsill if you live in a city, saying: "We give thanks for the harvest of the earth and for the harvest of good things in our lives."

Embrace or shake hands, saying: "We give thanks for each other." Finally, share among yourselves all your produce and home-baked dishes and enjoy them!

A solitary figure watches the sun set behind one of the wonders of the world—the Giza Pyramids, Eygpt.

Keeping Traditions Alive

At whatever time of the sacred year, and in whatever land these events take place, they all have one thing in common: they replay traditions that have been with us for hundreds, sometimes thousands of years. They remind us of our relationship to the summer sun, of its journey from May Day to harvest, and of our connection to the natural world, whose cycles of growth, blossoming, maturity, and decay mirror the seasons of our own lives.

Whether we choose simply to observe, or to go further and reenact these ancient ceremonies, by doing so, we take part in an age-old continuum of tradition and celebration and bring ourselves more fully into the sacred patterns of nature through which we live. What better way could there be to celebrate the glory of the sun, and the glory of our diverse and extraordinary cultures, than by acknowledging the power of the Summer Solstice, which affects us today just as it did our ancestors!

Additional Information

Further Reading

Alexander, Marc. *British Folklore, Myths and Legends.* London: Book Club Associates, 1982.

Aveni, Anthony. *Empires of Time: Calendars, Clocks and Cultures.* New York: Basic Books, 1989.

Bailey, Adrian. *The Caves of the Sun.* London: Jonathan Cape, 1997.

Blattmann, George. *The Sun.* Edinburgh: Floris Books, 1972.

Calvin, William H. *How the Shaman Stole the Moon.* New York: Bantam, 1991.

Cooper, Quentin, and Paul Sullivan. *Maypoles, Martyrs and Mayhem.* London: Bloomsbury, 1994.

Dames, Michael. *Mythic Ireland.* London: Thames & Hudson, 1992.

Dearmer, Percy, R. Vaughan Williams, and Martin Shaw. *The Oxford Book of Carols.* London: Oxford University Press, 1964.

Edwards, Carolyn McVickar. *Sun Stories.* San Francisco: HarperSanFrancisco, 1995.

Freeman, Mara. *Kindling the Celtic Spirit.* San Francisco: HarperSanFrancisco, 2000.

Gelling, Peter, and Hilda Ellis Davisdon. *The Chariot of the Sun.* London: J. M. Dent, 1969.

Green, Marian. *A Harvest of Festivals.* London: Longman, 1980.

Goulstone, John. *The Summer Solstice Games.* Privately printed, 1985.

Green, Miranda. *The Sun-Gods of Ancient Europe.* London: Batsford, 1991.

Hart, George. *A Dictionary of Egyptian Gods and Goddesses.* London: Routledge & Kegan Paul, 1986.

Heath, Robin. *Sun, Moon and Stonehenge.* Cardigan, Wales: Bluestone Press, 1998.

Heinberg, Richard. *Celebrate the Solstice.* Wheaton, Ill.: Quest Books, 1993.

Hunt, D. August. *The Road of the Sun.* Culver City, Cal.: Labyrinthos, 1997.

Hutton, Ronald. *The Stations of the Sun.* Oxford: Oxford University Press, 1996.

James, E. O. *Seasonal Feasts and Festivals.* London: Thames & Hudson, 1961.

Kane, Matt. *Heavens Unearthed in Nursery Rhymes and Fairy Tales.* Altoona, Penn.: Golden Egg Books, 1999.

Kightly, Charles. *The Customs and Ceremonies of Britain.* London: Thames & Hudson, 1986.

Kightly, Charles. *The Perpetual Almanack of Folklore.* London: Thames & Hudson, 1987.

Krupp, E .C. *Beyond the Blue Horizon.* New York: Harper Collins, 1991.

Krupp, E. C. *Skywatchers, Shamans and Kings.* New York: Wiley, 1997.

Lambeth, M. *A Golden Dolly: The Art, Mystery and History of Corn Dollies.* London: John Baker, 1969.

Leslie, Clare Walker, and Frank E. Gerace. *The Ancient Celtic Festivals and How We Celebrate Them Today.* Rochester Vt.: Inner Traditions, 2000.

Matthews, Caitlín. *Celtic Love: Ten Enchanted Stories.* San Francisco: HarperSanFrancisco, 2000.

Matthews, Caitlín. *The Celtic Spirit: Daily Meditations for the Turning Year.* San Francisco: Harper Collins, 1999. London: Hodder & Stoughton, 1999.

Matthews, Caitlín. *Elements of the Celtic Tradition.* Shaftesbury, Dorset: Element Books, 1989.

Matthews, John, and Caitlín Matthews. *The Winter Solstice.* New Alresford: Godsfield Press, 1998. Wheaton, Ill.: Quest Books, 1998.

Matthews, John. *The Quest for the Green Man.* New Alresford: Godsfield Press, 2001. Wheaton, Ill.: Quest Books, 2001.

Matthews, John *Robin Hood, Green Lord of the Wildwood.* Glastonbury, Somerset: Gothic Image Publications, 1993.

McCrickard, Janet. *Eclipse of the Sun: An Investigation of Sun and Moon Myths.* Glastonbury, Somerset: Gothic Image Publications, 1990.

McGrath, Sheena. *The Sun Goddess.* London: Blandford, 1997.

Olcott, W. T. *Sun Lore of All Ages.* New York and London: G. P. Putnams Sons, 1914. Reprinted Knickerbocker Press, 1999.

Poley, Jane, ed. *American Folk Lore and Legend.* Readers Digest Association, 1978.

Singh, Madanjeet. *The Sun in Myth and Art.* London: Thames & Hudson, 1998.

Whitlock, Ralph. *In Search of Lost Gods.* Oxford: Phaidon Press, 1969.

Organizations

THE REVELS
Leading the renaissance of solstice celebrations in the U.S.A. is Revels, a theatrical arts company inviting participation in performances nationwide. Established to promote traditional folk music and dance from around the world, Revels produces songbooks and how-to manuals for teachers and community leaders who wish to create May Day and other seasonal celebrations. CDs include two recordings for spring, *Wild Mountain Thyme*, and *Seasons for Singing*. See www.revels.org or contact the Revels office nearest you:

Boston, MA: Revels, Inc.
80 Mt. Auburn Street
Watertown, MA 02472
Tel: 617-972-8300
Fax: 617-972-8400
E-Mail: info@revels.org

Boulder, CO: (303) 447-1919
stevejoew@aol.com

Evanston, IL: (312) 409-3834
revelschicago@aol.com

Hanover, NH: (603) 298-8913
stalker@cyberportal.net

Houston, TX: (713) 668-3303
revelshou@iapc.net

New York, NY: info@nyrevels.org

Oakland, CA: (510) 452-9334
calrevels@calrevels.org

Philadelphia, PA: (610) 949-9410
d.darragh@home.com

Portland, OR: (503) 224-7411
lewisdik@aol.com

St. Paul, MN: (612) 724-9240
mn_revels@yahoo.com

Tacoma, WA: (253) 756-1804
psrevels@aol.com

Washington, DC: (202) 723-7528
info@revelsdc.org

The English Folk Song and Dance Society
2, Regents Park Road
London NW1 7AY, U.K.
www.efdss.org

A CD of music to accompany this book will be available from High Bohemia Records.
www.martinsimpson.com

Index

A

Abbots Bromley Horn Dance 139
Aborigines 49
Aesir 54
agriculture 106
Alfrodull 49
Amatarasu 21
America 22, 25, 46–7, 117
Amon-Ra 18
Anake 76
Anasazi 22, 134
ancestors 6–7, 10–12, 15–16, 141
Ankor Wat 18–20
Apalachees 46–7
Aphrodite 109
Apollo 42–5, 69, 73, 109
architecture 12
Ares 109
Aristarchus of Samos 10
Aristotle 11
Artemis 42, 109
Arthur, King 73, 90
astronomy 12, 18–21, 86
Aten 40–1
Athena 12, 108–9
Attis 75, 77
August 138–41
Australia 49
Aztecs 25

B

Baal Fire 137
Baja 134
Balder 54
Bali 121
Baltic region 49, 56
Barnwell Priory 86
Bavarian Summer Festival 137
Bede's Well 87
Bel 137
Belenus 66, 69
Bella Cool Indians 17
Beltaine 66–79
birching 71
blessings 61, 62, 80
Blodeuwedd 77
Bone Fire 98
Borneo 119
Boudicca, Queen 135
Brahmins 20
bread 124
Breide Ogg 113
Bridget 113
Britain 13
    festivals 128–33, 137–8
    Harvest 114, 121
    May 68–70, 79
    Midsummer 86, 94
Bronze Age 38–9
Burma 120

C

Cadbury Castle 90
Cailleach 113
Calanish 88
calendar 126–41
Cambodia 18–19
Camdem 70
Canada 17
Canute, Laws of 96
Carmichael, Alexander 97, 112
Carrack Sans 87
Cassivelaunus, King 68
Castleton 133
Caucasian Mountains 13
celebrations 6–7
    festivals 133–4, 140–1
    Harvest 106
    May 73–5, 79
    Midsummer 86, 89–90, 96, 99–102
Celts 13–14, 39, 54
    festivals 135, 137–8
    Harvest 116–17
    May 66, 68, 71, 73
    Midsummer 87
Central America 25
Cerne Abbas Giant 88
Chaco Canyon 134
Charles I, King 138
Charles II, King 133
Chartres Cathedral 134
Chichen Itza 25
China 10, 20–1
Christianity 44–7, 54
    festivals 140
    Harvest 121
    May 69, 73–4, 76, 80
    Midsummer 96–9
Comical Pilgrim 96–7
Constantine, Emperor 44, 73
Copernicus, Nicholas 11
Coricancha 25
Corn Dance 140
corn dolls 113, 117–18, 122
Corn Palace Festival 139
Cuchulainn 54
Cuzco 25
Cybele 75, 77
cycles 6–7, 16–17, 76, 111
Czech Republic 128

D

Dakota people 47
damson and apple tansey 124
dancing
    festivals 133, 138–40
    Harvest 117–18
    May 66, 82
    Midsummer 88, 99, 101
darkness 34
Deling's Dore 17
Delos 42
Delphi 42–3
Demeter 109–11
deosil 12

Devil's Arrows 88
Diana 42
Diodorus Siculus 69
Dionysus 109
divination 94–5
dords 10
dragon energy 99
dreams 136
Druids 10, 13, 135–6

E

Earth's axis 14–15
eastern festivals 20–1
Edgar, King 96
Edward VI, King 74
Egypt 16–17, 18, 38, 40–1, 106, 139
Eleusinian festivals 110–21
Elgin Marbles 109
equinoxes 20–2, 25, 75
Eros 109

F

fairies 71–3, 92–4, 101, 131, 136
fairs 74, 86, 88, 134, 138–9
fall festivals 139
Feast of the Tabernacles 139
ferns 94
fertility rites 76, 88, 95, 112
festivals 13–14
    calendar 126–41
    Harvest 108, 110–21
    May 68–9, 73, 75
    Midsummer 88, 96–102
Finland 94, 114–15
Fionn mac Cumhail 72
fire 12–14, 20
    festivals 134, 136–7
    May 66–79
    Midsummer 86–102
Flora 77, 128, 132
flowers 95, 133
Forbidden City 21
France 14, 45
    festivals 128, 130, 134
    Midsummer 95, 98
Furry Day Carol 132–3

G

El-Gabal 43
Galilei, Galileo 11
games 89–90, 106, 108–9
Garland King Day 133
garlands 80, 90, 133
Gawain 54
Gawthorpe 132
Geoffrey of Monmouth 68
Germany 14, 95, 128
ghosts 72, 97
Gilgamesh 40, 54
gnomons 20, 25
gods 16–17, 32, 38–53, 106–24
Golowan Festival 99
Great Feather Dance 140
Great Spirit 25–6

Greeks 12, 42–3, 54
    festivals 128
    Harvest 110–11, 117
    May 69, 72
Green Corn Festival 139–40
Green Man 77, 91, 138
Gregory the Great, Pope 96
Grindall, Archbishop 91
Guatemala 25
guided imagery 60
Gwydion 77

H

Hades 110
Halley's Comet 21
Harvest 12, 104–24, 138, 140–1
Hawaii 128
hele stone 10
heliocentric universe 10–11
Heliopolis 40
Helston 132
Hephaestus 109
Hera 42, 45, 109
Hercules 54
Hermes 109
heroes 54
hills 86–102
Hinduism 20
hobby-horses 114, 139
holidays 6
Hopi 22
Hull, Eleanor 131
hymns 41, 47, 121

I

Iceland 13
Incas 25
Independence Day 137
India 10
Indonesia 119, 121
Inuit 13, 28
Ireland 13–14, 38–9, 54
    festivals 135
    Harvest 113
    May 70
    Midsummer 94, 96
Iroquois 46, 117, 139
Isis 106
Isle of Man 131
Italy 128
Ivy Girl 113

J

Japan 21
Java 121
John Barleycorn 106–8
Jubilee College Park 134
Judaism 15–16, 138–9
Julian, Emperor 99
Julius Caesar 68
July 137
June 134–6

K

Kachinas 22
Kalvaitis 56–9